THE 256 ODÙ OF IFA

CUBAN AND TRADITIONAL

VOL. 5

Ògbè Ògúnda-Ògbè Òsá

MARCELO MADAN

i

NOTE TO THIS EDITION

As we have already noticed in our previous Ifá literatures, it is about transcription of manuscript documents, many of them unpublished, with different wording and literary styles, I have always tried to keep in essence, the idea of what was wanted to express, for Therefore, it is quite difficult to achieve uniformity of style in this regard. In this new presentation I show in each of the Odù, everything from the literature of Afro-Cuban Ifá and traditional African Ifá.

It is in my interest, to provide Ifá students this time, a broad vision in all its dimensions of what Ifá can encompass, taking into account, in addition, that what is presented in this is not everything, because Ifá is much deeper. and his literary work is much more abundant than what I show here, this is only a part, even when I have added to these volumes' concepts from the previously published ifá treatises, as well as traditional ifá. In addition, it is not my intention here to suggest any kind of supremacy between the two trends, only to show them as each of them is presented and that it is the reader himself who judges and prefers its future use. My aim is to offer you the possibility of having at hand, a renewed tool for study, broader and more effective that allows you at the same time, to enter the learning of both literatures without limitations or discrimination, each one in its field, because ultimately, the knowledge of Ifá is universal and is for everyone alike.

GRATEFULNESS

Thanks to Olódùmarè, for having enlightened me and allow to create this work, to be able to throw the light of knowledge to everyone who needs it.

Thanks to Òrúnmìlà spirit of light that guides me and takes me along the right path.

Thanks to Obatala, my guard angel who always accompanies me and provides timely protection.

Thanks to my maternal grandmother and godmother Rosa Torrez (Ṣàngó Womí)

Thanks to my godfather Rubén Pineda Baba Ejìògbè

CONTENT

1- OGBÈ ÒGÚNDÁ; OGBÈ ÌYỌ́NÚ; OGBÈ ÌYÀMI

+

I I
I I
I I
O I

I PRAY:

Ògbè Iyonu Aya adé mo wá jé ere ni laye A dífá fún Oodùa wá jé ni efa ewa jé Odùdúwà Ikú si gbe rè, Àrùn si gbe rè, Òfò si gbe rè, Eyó si gbe rè, Ogu si gbe rè, Onilú si gbe rè, Àṣelú si gbe rè

Ìyere

Atiponla ifá duuru (4 times)

Ifá owó, Ifá Ìmó, ifá iré atiponla ifá duuru

PRAY 2:

Màrìwò Ọpẹ̀ já sòòrò kanlè; Díá fún wọn n'Ílalà; Níbi ojú gbé mọ́ Ire

Translation:

A new palm frond shoot is straight from the base tip; He was the one who launched ifá for the citizens of the town of

Ílalǎ; Where days of anger normally dawn.

- Ifá says that he foresees an ire of happiness and worldly successes for the client for whom this odú is revealed.
- Ifá says that he will not allow pain due to bad experiences or disappointment.

IFÁ OF:

- Treason
- Impact

PROVERBS:

- Open your mouth, talk dirty, and calm your hunger
- The sheep are still wearing their wool from last year.
- The best fortune; The having, the power and the knowledge
- The sweet tooth enlarges the belly and shrinks its head
- Goat that breaks a drum with its hide pays
- As crocodiles live in the river, so Ògbè Iyonu will be eternal
- The sheep that is associated with a dog will eat shit
- He who carries a candle in his hands, cannot wait
- He who commits adultery with a man's wife will always be his enemy.
- We find money in the world, and we leave it in the world
- Man makes a young man an old man, a full belly makes a young man old
- The eye does not kill the bird
- When the wild goat is alive, the hide cannot be used for a drum, but when it dies, no one hesitates to use its hide as a

2

drum.

- I travel the world, this is what Olófin told Odùdúwà

BORN:

- The Ẹbọ Ṣiré
- Why, Òṣùn is offered a gelding
- The Ifá mallet necklace (Iñafá)
- Hooks from the butcher shop
- The molars
- Ayalá Ọbàtàlá builder of heads and receives offerings in sacrifices
- The unification of the world and the union of human beings.
- The filling of the teeth
- Putting the Egúngún from Eegún to Elégbà
- Pancreas alterations.
- The taking of the position Ekobí Enyobí Abakua
- That this is where the dead were not buried
- Let him touch his head with the Òpèlè and the inkines to guess the people
- That they did Ifá to Bàbálú Ayé and he was called Olúwo Popo
- Settling Òṣà for the first time
- Birth of Ògún Ṣiro Ṣero
- The water reservoir (The dam)

BRAND

- Impotence

3

• Stomach problem.

SIGNALIZE

• Of three surgical operations and difficulties in the eye.

IFÁ SAYS

• Speaks: Şàngó, Odùdúwà, Olúwo Popó, y Òşùn
• Of alteration of the Pancreas.
• That the person can be impotent and suffer a shame due to sexual laziness.
• Of lack of respect and offenses in the marriage of both parties, since her husband does not interest her as a man.
• The great thief: He lives and enjoys state assets, he is the great embezzler of the public purse.
• Out of embarrassment and that you, out of pride, can use a weapon and have a misfortune
• There is opposition in love relationships
• From strokes, viruses, colitis, operations, pressure and the heart
• That the person is down and the enemies laugh
• From stomach problems, product of ailments in the mouth
• Of dismantling an Altar and for that reason they have delay
• Separation and distancing. It is solved with two Àkúko funfun (path of the unification of the lands)
• Gluttony so you must respect the alligator
• Of tragedy and anger where weapons have been used and they are imprisoned or will be.
• From being one-eyed or sick in one eye

- Of the death of a child

PROHIBITIONS

- The son of this Ifá should never eat Pigeons again in his life
- You cannot drink alcoholic beverages
- Do not hit any woman

RECOMMENDATIONS

- Take care of the teeth in your mouth and stomach and go to the doctor
- Receive Brosia
- When Awo sees this sign, that day he does not sit at the table
- Do Ẹbọ to avoid future impotence problems
- Make Ẹbọ so that you can go to another place and not go to prison
- Beware of strokes, colitis, viruses, operations, pressure and the heart.
- Be careful not to become a slave to those who are your slaves today
- Take care of your house and do not fight with your spouse, so that you reach the luck
- Receive Elégbà first and then complete the rest
- Respect the Cayman and do not be gluttonous or greedy
- Do not fight with your wife, or throw him out on the street, because you may regret it

EWÉ ODÙ OGBÈ ÒGÚNDÀ

Jobo--Olobotuye—Atiponlá---Sigüaraya

For more information see: Encyclopedia of Ifá herbs by Marcelo Madan

PÀTAKI LISTING

1. The union of human beings
2. The three brothers (when you go to travel consult Ifá)
3. With patience he becomes king
4. Ògbè Iyonu is Orí omí Ìkokò
5. Where the awunko was mounted
6. Òşùn's luck
7. Why eats Òşùn a castrated goat
8. Impotence.
9. Where the dead were not buried

WORKS WITH OGBÈ ÒGÚNDÀ

Secret of Ògbè Iyono: Odùdúwà Agusu wears a silver Ilú (little drum) adorned with ìleké and goes inside Odùdúwà's chest.

For the stomach:

Mamú cooking of ewé Yiní (cundiamor), with water from the container of Òşùn and eni.

Artwork by Ògbè Iyonu to clean your teeth.

Take a long guava toothpick, with a sharp point; on a plate, paint Osé Òtùrà, Ògbè Iyonu, Òtùrà Sé and on top of that, put the toothpick and give it food with Elégbà and sing:

" afafa bokino fatawao made ".

Then the teeth are cleaned with that stick.

Work to raise the health of Ògbè Iyonú.

16 eiyelé funfun and eight Awo are needed. Each Awo takes two eiyelé and with them, when uniting, they cover the lerí de Ògbè Iyonu and each one of them prays two méjì de Ifá.

Afterwards, he is made sarayeye with all the eiyelé, which are given to Obàtàlá.

Work to remove a disturbing Eegún from the ilé.

You take an igba with omí and add pieces of Işu (yam) and put it behind the shilekun ilé, you also add a little piece of banana strain and iyefá. With a gio-gio everyone is cleansed and sacrifices himself together with the igba, casting eyebale inside. The contents of the igba are then sprinkled throughout the house, first crushing the contents of the igba and the gio-gio ará and adding epó. Later everything is collected and a package is made that is carried to the foot of a Cardón bush, calling Azowano well.

Gio-gio   Cardón   Ewé Yini Cundeamor)

Èṣù AGELO

This Èṣù rides on a stuffed alligator that takes care of Ogbè Yono's house. He lives planted in an Ikokó with: Land from the cemetery, plowed land, 4 inkines, Ilèakan, land from a lagoon, from the river, from the sea, from a slaughterhouse, from a prison, a bush and a Lamí-Lamí (seahorse) , akokàn, Oyú and lerí from Àkúko, 3 alligator tusks, erú, obí, kolá, osun, alligator leather, 21 ataré, 21 òtá kéke bald Chinese, 21 òtá kéke from the coast or beach, prodigious, fine grass, bledo colorado, ewe goosefoot, male fern, ceiba root, red mangrove, jagüey, handsome amansa, winner, win war, win battle, for me, Yamao, change voice, three jets, three corals, three amber, gold and silver. They put eyes and mouths of snails, blades with jujú from ikóodíde and Gungun. A small necklace with Piñón seeds is put on it, an aṣeré is made of mamey seeds that are filled with alligator bones to touch it. It is surrounded by a chain.

Òsányin of Ogbè Yono (way of Asójaanú).

Lerí of Ẹtu, of Asójaanú (he wonders how many), an aguoná, aparó, corojos (he wonders how many), Bibijagua land, Iyefá of Ogbè Yono not prayed, and he wonders how many strong sticks and which ones they are.

Işé of Ogbè Yono:

A goat is given to Elégbà, the meat is distributed in the jungle, a stool is lined with the skin to sit on a doll, a piece of the skin is taken to cover an Işé de Òsányin and the rest is used as an Elégbà rug, of the jars are loaded to put it to Ògún.

For impotence

Mamu, red mangrove tisane, mastuerzo leaves and Cobo snail marrow, drink as common water.

Işé of Òsányin

Iye de lerí de Àkúko, adié, lands of different colors, inso of Tiger or Leopard, gbogbo igi, obí motiguao, obí, Edun, orugbo, Eru, aíra, eku, epo, àgbado.

For the stomach

Mamu(take) decoctions of ewe Yini (cundeamor), with water from the tureen of Òşùn y eñi

Work for iré Umbo

An Owunko is given to Elégbà and its meats are distributed in the mountain, with the skin a rhaetian taboo is lined to seat an Ebora, with the bags of that skin an Işé of Òsányin is loaded and a piece to put it as a carpet Elegba. The jars are

9

loaded and put to Ògún.

Work with which Asójaanú saved Òrúnmìlà when Kukutu came to eat him

Òrúnmìlà is given a plate with 16 branches of holy basil and on Friday before 12 o'clock an ẹbọmisi is prepared with that basil, efún, raw Wara Malu, eri, Iyefá del Odù to bathe, after having given the 6 in the afternoon, one Jutía and two ẹtu to Asójaanú.

Work of Ogbè Iono to clean your teeth

Take a small long guava stick, with a sharp tip, paint Oṣe Otùrà, Ogbè Iono, Òtùrà Òṣé on a plate and put the stick on top and give it food with Elégbà and sing: Afafa Bokino Fatawao Made. Then the teeth are cleaned with that toothpick.

Ẹbomisí to attract Obírin and to attract ọkọnrin

Leaves of: Yamao, for me, open paths, Reseda, Sacu-sacu, Poppy, do not forget me, Pega Pollo (Chicken Paste), victor, Cinnamon, Oyin and river and rain water

Work to improve the health of Ogbè Yono

16 Ẹiyelé funfun and 8 Awo are needed, each one takes two Ẹiyelé and with them when joined they cover Ogbè Yono's lerí and each one of the Awo prays two méjìs of Ifá, then they make Sarayeye with all the Ẹiyelé, which are given to Obatala

10

Work to remove an Eegún from the ilè

Take an igba with omí and add a bit of Işu and put it behind şilikun Ilè, also add a bit of banana strain and Iyefá, with a gio-gio everyone present is cleaned and killed along with the igba by pouring eyebale into it, then the content of the igba is sprinkled throughout the house, first crushing the content of the igba and the ara of the gio-gio and pouring epo on it, then everything is collected and a ball is made that is taken to the foot of a Cardón bush calling Asójaanú.

Secret of Ogbè Iono

Odùdúwà Agusu carries a silver Ilú (little drum) adorned with ìleké and goes inside Odùdúwà's chest.

OGBÈ YONO PÀTAKI 1 THEUNIFICATION OF THE WORLD AND THE UNION OF HUMAN BEINGS.

I PRAY:

Ogbè Yono obo nilo osabo Ogbè Yono obo nile sabe aboni lara awo fe şe iré bobo lerí mọ lala ji re awo ifá unlo yeba meni lala aberi láye bobo ni je re òbàrà dada ifá lade tinşe me awo ni alara Ogbè Yono ọba ti obo ifá láye nifá ọmọ lala nifá ọmọ lala Ogbè Yono ifá nifá be aşegun òtá ifá ọmọ lade káfírèfún Òrúnmìlà ifá káfírèfún Ògún káfírèfún Şàngó.

ĘBỌ:

Àkúko funfun, gbogbo lerí, gbogbo jujú, gbogbo agbo,

11

gbogbo aro, gbogbo Inlé, gbogbo eran, gbogbo Tenujen, erú, epó, Àgbado, gbogbo ìleké y gbogbo ewé.

Pàtaki:

Before, human beings and the earth lived separately from each other. Olofin lived for that very sad and self-conscious, seeing the disunity that existed between men. The one who did not have to eat was left without eating because nobody gave him a piece of bread, nor helped him.

Òbàtála who was also very sad for that reason went to see Olófin, they began to talk about this situation and reached a conclusion, it was necessary to send for Ṣàngó to fix this situation. Òbàtála went out in search of Ṣàngó, but the one he found was Òrúnmìlà, after telling him how upset Olofin was and the agreement made, Òrúnmìlà took out the Òpèle and saw this Odù and told him: Not only do you have to look for Ṣàngó but also to Ògún, but before going to look for him it is necessary to put Eran and Ògún's ìtanná behind Olófin's door, after in fact they went looking for him and were singing: Ogbè Yono Ogbara, ọba Odeo, ni Ṣàngó aguo Ọmọ Ògún ala guedeo.

Ògún and Ṣàngó lived opposite each other, one in their land when they saw who was approaching, they ran to meet them and hugged each other, then they told them, this union that you have made is what we need in the world, so that life be more pleasant and better shared among all, so that Olofin lives a little calmer and happier. Hearing this, the answer was not long in coming, Ṣàngó said: We will try by all means and with the help of all the forces of the different lands to unite, and thus human beings live more peacefully, but there will always be difficulties, envy, ambition and the war between each other. In the world, Ṣàngó continued, it cannot be like you, that is how human being's end. Ogun and I will make some union exist and we will seek that some human beings share their things with others. So, they prepared to return to Olófin's house, along the way they were collecting a little earth from each one of them, as well as the things and products that were in each one of them, while they walked Òbàtála told Òrúnmìlà that his judgment was missing something, at that moment Òrúnmìlà saw that there was Àkúko funfun and he took it. Arriving at Olófin's house, Òrúnmìlà sat down and prayed to Ṣàngó and Ògún fed him Àkúko funfun and then they were happy to look for some humans to teach them good, so Ṣàngó with his word and Ògún with his strength achieved it with some people.

OGBÈ YONO PÀTAKI 2: WHEN YOU GO TO TRAVEL, CONSULT WITH ÒRÚNMÌLÀ (The three brothers)

I PRAY:

Adífáfún Ayedogun Adífáfún Okànkan Adífáfún Hoalale.

Pàtaki

There was a man who died leaving three children and they had to go to collect the inheritance to a land that was

13

separated from it by the sea and they had to make the trip by boat. The first went to Òrúnmìlà's house and he made osode for him and marked ẹbọ but he did not want to do it and decided to embark with his wife without doing so, he embarked on a ship whose captain liked to take women from travelers and as soon as the captain he saw Okakan's wife he took her and dishonored her then Okakan claimed the captain and he killed him.

The second also went to Òrúnmìlà's house and told him the same thing, but he didn't want to do the ẹbọ either, and when he boarded the ship, the same thing happened to him as to his brother. The third was where Òrúnmìlà marked the ẹbọ for him and he also did it. Òrúnmìlà also recommended that when he embarked with his wife, he should take the maid with his wife's clothes and the woman with the maid's clothes and that when something happened not would claim anything. The boy made the ẹbọ with a rooster, 3 pesos, a real, and a half, and the other ingredients and then he embarked.

The same thing happened, which instead of happening to the woman happened to the maid and since there was no claim, he was able to reach his destination.

When Ayodogui arrived at his destination they crowned him king of those lands and the court asked him if he wanted anything else after the coronation, they asked him if he had no enemies or if no one had offended him, to which he

14

replied that the only His enemy was the captain of the ship that had taken him to those lands and who had offended him morally, telling his brothers what had happened and the fate they had suffered. Then he ordered that the captain be brought to his presence. As soon as he arrived, he immediately recognized his former passenger and became very frightened during the interrogation. He said where the two women who were princesses of the court were and who were on his ship. They sent for the two princesses and the king told the captain, you will be killed, and then burned and your ashes will be scattered over the sea so that all who are like you learn their lesson.

The two princesses were received with all the ceremonies and all the grandeur they deserved and they stayed to live in the palace next to their brother-in-law. When you go to travel, see yourself with Òrúnmìlà and do the works that mark him so that he can arrive well at his destination.

OGBÈ YONO PÀTAKI 3: WITH PATIENCE BECOMES KING.

Pàtaki

Aya was a beautiful Serpent who performed all kinds of miracles. She changed into my wife, she married Vodun Anjaca. One day, he was absent and asks his wife to prepare food for him. When he was left alone, he took his cane and his hat and his things, she told him: What you left me, I had to take it to make the fire to cook, convinced Anjuaca, who would never get his clothes back, repudiates his wife, she leaves and meets Komoso and starts living with him, the same thing happened to her as with Anjuaca and he dumped her.

Ifá was preparing the annual ceremonies, it recorded when the sign of Ogbè Yono came, where Elégbà announces: "This year will be good for everyone, you will marry more, to keep your wife with you, you will have to arm yourself with a lot of patience". 32 days later, a beautiful and flirtatious woman enters her house and he asks her why do you come? To be your wife, she says, he tells her, it's you and he married her.

Ifá had never married and Aja was his first wife, one day he asked her to eat because he would go out, she takes her husband's tie, breaks it into pieces and makes fire with it, Ifá came and ate and left nothing, she left Again, she burned all her Ifá belongings and killed all her animals.

15 days after the ceremony, she told Ifá: Everything is different, how will you do it? He told her: Don't worry, he had a board carved and bought the animals again, then Aja thought, I've hurt this man and he's doing me good and told him, I'm going to defecate, take me to the tomb of your father, he defecated a lot of gold there, how the other husbands did not defecate. Eight days later, she told him at night, Ifá I am going to defecate, he told her, you know the way, yes, she said, but this time it will be in your mother's grave, she went and defecated silver and precious stones.

16

One night when he was with her, he told her, look, I didn't want to cheat on you, I had two husbands before and because of my wickedness they left me, I burned your board, I killed your animals and you didn't get angry with me, that's why I defecated in the tomb of your father and nothing, I will give you children that I carry in my womb, go to the graves of your parents and take everything that belongs to you there. She gave him as sons Amosun, Raka, Alughakevo. That is why his wives give their riches to Ifá.

OGBÈ YONO PÀTAKI 4: OGBÈ YONO IS ORÍ OMÍ IKOKO.

I PRAY:

Bábà Ogbè oro Ogunda orí yanyan Ikokó Òrùn agbada alawó adífáfún Awó unikoko awo bonu omo Ogbè Yono Oluwo Popo. Awantefa odara Ikokó toşe Olókun olori burukú ku loso ya aku niko omo Ogbè Ogunda Ikokó kombe loyu Orí adenifá Elégbà oba badon omisisikikin ewé onikoko ape Awó omo awan omo nifá.

EBO:

Àkúko, gio-gio, adié méjì, gbogbo àşe, atitan Inlé, Ikokó, eleguede, Işu, ekú, eja, Àgbado, obí, otín, epó, ìtanná, orí, efún, awankéké, mariwo, gbogbo ìleké, gbogbo Eré, gbogbo ewéfá, aşoburú funfun y opolopo owó.

17

<u>Note:</u>

The ẹbọ goes in the basket, but it is first washed with omiero and given the gio-gio and added to Òrúnmìlà. The eye is thrown into the ẹbọ and the omiero. The Àkúko is given to Elégbà and the eyé is also given to the ẹbọ and the omiero, the person bathes with the omiero, then the pot keeps it. The remaining ewéfá is taken along with the gio-gio to the sea.

Pàtaki

Awó Ikokó who was Ọmọ Ogbè Yono lived in the Awó Bonu and lived comfortably, he was always feeding Olókun. He brought her food cooked in a large pot and raw in a basket and sang to her: Olókun awankameme lodo Awó Ilè Ogbè Yono Ikokó Alaṣenifá.

Then Olokun would come out and give him his blessing.

In that land, people dedicated themselves to making Ikokó out of clay and it had been a long time since anyone was consecrated in Ifá. Awó onikokó was getting old and always told the people of Awó bonu that to worship Olokun one had to have ifá consecration.

One day Olókun told him, you are no longer for these trajines, go looking for one to consecrate it in ifá. Awó ikokó began to look for him, but since the people of that land did not walk with ifá, they were only there to make ikokó, he did not find any that he thought would serve and in that he set

18

out to Olókun's house, to bring him his food. Along the way he met ọmọ Olókun and said to himself: This will be the one who will serve me to consecrate him, so that the people of this land think a little more about ifá, then he said to ọmọ Olókun: I am going to consecrate you in ifá to that you help me keep this land prosperous as it is now and so that they think more about ifá and Olókun was very happy and gave everything to Ogbè Yono (Awó onikokó), so that he could consecrate his son. Awó onikokó began to prepare everything and when they were going to Oloya to buy some things to eat, he met Elégbà and Oluwo Popo. Elégbà had two large and new Ikokó and Oluwo Popo a very large awan and gbogbo eye. They gave Mo fori bale to Awó onikokó and told him: We were waiting for you to give you what you need, to consecrate the Ọmọ Olókun. Then Oluwo Popo gave him the awan and told him: Put everything you need here, but first, you have to consecrate yourself; take gbogbo ewé ni latefa and wash the awan inside and out, sacrifice the gio-gio against the awan inside and give him the eye on the outside and say: ọmọ Adié, ọmọ Enifá, Òrùn Awan, throw the gio-gio in the corner. Then he knelt in front of Elégbà and he gave him the two Ikokó and told him: These are, one of your head and the other, the head of the ọmọ Olókun your son who is going to be born and he gave them to him and prayed to him:

Òsányinawo onikokó Agaba Alaṣenifá

and told him: make the omiero and when he prepares it, give

19

him a ẹiyelé and sing:

Òyèkú niye kure, Òyèkú Niye Kure, ibo ẹiyelé Òsányin ibo.

And light one ìtanná, the other Ikokó, you put it inside the awan along with everything else and cover it with Aṣọ funfun and pray:

Akuré ifá kun- kun awan atenifá.

Everything was already prepared for the consecration, they took the awan out and began to sing:

Awan, Awan koṣe wa run Awan oni kokó Enifá alawó awan.

Then Elégbà, Oluwo Popo, Awó onikokó y gbogbo Awó they sang:

Awan ọmọnifá umbo awan ifá

and they took him to Ibodun, where he was consecrated and took out Ogbè Yono, Elégbà told him: Keep that Ikokó of the awan, for another secret that this land lacks, that is, the Obé so that everything goes well for him and for you, then many people from Awó Bonu arrived so that Awó onikokó and Awó ọmọ Olókun consecrated them in ifá. Olókun was very happy and sent riches to both of them, her son was Ogbè Yono ifá Bonu. The people thought more about ifá and used the pots in sacred things, because they were the heads of that land of Awó Bonu ifá Bonu.

Note: The pots of atefar must always be new, since they are

20

presented in the head of the godfather and the godson, the pot that is given to the godson is the basket, which he will take to work until he takes kuanaldo, since this is the one that breaks in the kutun.

Since then, Ogbè Yono is Orí Oní Ikokó.

OGBÈ YONO PÀTAKI 5 WHERE THE AWUNKO WAS MOUNTED (BIG GOAT).

Pàtaki

On his way to the land of Dahomey, ọmọlú took a long time to arrive, he crossed the long wild road, then in the town of Şaki he met an Ayaba from that city called Ottanogoso, the one who had many big and bearded Òbúko, who served as horse in those places and she, seeing him so tired, offered Ogbè Yono who was the guide of ọmọlú, an Òbúko to continue the trip and gave him a badge so that wherever he arrived, his servants would offer him presents and a fresh Òbúko.

These accounts of his ìleké in the ja and how beautiful stones from his kingdom that identified him as Ayaba de Şaki, made up the insignia he gave him. The trip from Şaki to saya took five days, five posts passed and in each one of them, when showing the insignia, he received from Ottanogoso's servants, great gifts of fruits and snails with Ogbè Yono, from then until his coronation in Dahomey, each day his fame and power of ọmọlú, which was later titled Asojano,

21

was greater, for this reason the secret of Ogbè Yono is to give five Òbúko to Òṣùn to be great. For this reason, the Asojano vodeunsi mount the Òbúko in their ceremony in memory of the horse he rode from Ṣaki to Saye, and the Awó gives him the Òbúko ridden by the vodeunsi, circling the yardua five times before mounting it in memory of the five days that Ogbè Yono and Asojano surrendered, as a guide and the other as a rider from Ṣaki to Saye.

OGBÈ YONO PÀTAKI 6: OṢUN'S LUCK.

Pàtaki

When Òṣùn went to Òrúnmìlà's house to register, Òrúnmìlà made him bear seeing this ifá and marked him ẹbọ with: 5 Àkúko, adié, pumpkin, other ingredients. And if she moved an Àkúko, that was where her luck came and Òrúnmìlà married her.

OGBÈ YONO PÀTAKI 7: HE WHY OṢUN EATS CASTRATED GOAT.

Pàtaki

It turns out that when Adié lived with Òrúnmìlà and Òṣùn as his wife, he had promised his wife that if she died, he would not have women and that he would castrate himself. Shortly after they talked about this, Òṣùn died, becoming a river, time passed and Òrúnmìlà did not fulfill her commitment. One day Òsányin sang to Òrúnmìlà: Okurinkuel Ekó Adifá Ekó Òṣùn and he reminded Òṣùn of

22

his oath. Then osode was made and this ifá was seen, where Òṣùn claimed his debt, Ifá told him to buy an Òbúko, castrate it and wrap the okó in his underpants and take it to Alakaso so that he would take it to Olofin as proof of the fulfillment of his promise, and that he promulgates it to the four winds that he, Òrúnmìlà, was sick, that later he would take the Òbúko, dress it with his clothes and give it to Ibú, so that

Òṣùn received it.

Òrúnmìlà did so, and Òṣùn was satisfied and since then it is offered to Òṣùn the castrated Goat.

OGBÈ YONO PÀTAKI 8: IMPOTENCE.

Pàtaki

It was a kingdom in which ọba had all his subjects subjugated and he thought that the more subjects he had, the easier it would be for him to remain sovereign, one day he ordered that all the male subjects be castrated.

There was a marriage, the man was called Yumurí and he lived in a cave and the king's soldiers arrived there, as he refused to be castrated, the soldiers in revenge cut off his penis, leaving him emasculated.

One day Òrúnmìlà arrived in that land and met Yumurí, who told him what the soldiers of King Òrúnmìlà had done to him, made him bear and saw this ifá and took a snail and

23

with the bug from it he formed Yumurí's penis and with àṣe he hit it, then he put Òbúko's testicles on it and with the Bábà of the bug Cobo, he gave it a drink so that it would transform into semen.

So Yumurí returned to ofikale trupon with his Obìrin with whom shortly after he had a son. One day the king found out that Yumurí had a son and replied that that could not be since I myself saw when my soldiers emasculated and castrated him, given the persistence of such a rumor the King one day said: Let's go see Yumurí and if it's true that your wife has a son, I'll pay with my head.

When the King was before Yumurí, they verified the truth and those who accompanied him reminded him of his oath and the ọba killed himself.

Note:

The person has a defect in his genital system that leads to impotence.

OGBÈ YONO PÀTAKI 9: WHERE THE DEAD WERE NOT BURIED.

Pàtaki

In the Arará land there was a great mortality and the tribe was being decimated. Òrúnmìlà went to that place and the King told him about the case and he made him ẹbọ with: Pico, guataca, shovel, efún sack, Àkúko. After finishing the

24

ẹbọ, with those tools he would open a large ditch burying all the dead (because the dead were not buried there). Afterwards, it was ordered that all the houses be painted white with the efun. After this operation was over, great downpours fell, and he had recommended that no one get wet. And so, the epidemic disappeared from that place. And in such virtue the Arará will perform all his work at the foot of Òrúnmìlà.

2- TRADITIONAL IFÁ OGBE OGUNDA

OGBE OGUNDA VERSE 1

Màrìwò Òpè já sòòrò kanlè;

Díá fún won n'Ílalà;

Níbi ojú gbé mó Ire.

Translation:

A new palm frond shoot is straight from the base tip

He was the one who launched Ifá for the citizens of the town of ílalà

Where days of anger normally dawn.

PROPHECY

Ifá says that he foresees the ire of happiness and worldly successes for the client for whom this odú is revealed. Ifá says that Ifá does not allow this client to experience pain or disappointment.

Pàtaki

The people of the town of ílalà approached the Babalawo

whose pseudonym was "a recently the sprout frond is straight from the base point" for Ifá consultation. They want to determine whether or not the town of ílalà is a prosperous town for all They also wanted to know if all the citizens of ílalà did not suffer long before acquiring all the ire of life such as a husband, wealth, children, longevity and so on.

The Babaláwos reported that they would never experience pain in the town of ílalà. He said every morning when they woke up. The spirits responsible for the entire ire of life would converge to give them whatever they required. They were then asked to offer sacrifice with three roosters, three hens, three guinea fowl and money. They complied.

Before long, the town of ílalà became very pleasant. All the citizens were happy and prosperous. Those in need of money became wealthy, those in need of a husband got convenient, those in need of children were able to deliver their children without trouble and they lived long. They were all dancing and singing and very happy. They were also praising their awo.

Màrìwò Òpè já sòòrò kanlè;
Díá fún won n'Ílalà;
Níbi ojú gbé mó Ire. Ojú Ire mó mi l´´onìí;
Mo lówó lówó;
Màrìwò Òpè já sòòrò kanlè;
Ì wo má lawo ojúmó Ire;
Ojú Ire mó mi lónìí; Mo láya nílé;
Màrìwò Òpè já sòòrò kanlè;
Ì wo má lawo ojúmó Ire;

28

Ojú Ire mó mi lónìí;
Mo bímo lémo; Màrìwò Òpè já sòòrò kanlè;
Ì wo má lawo ojúmó Ire o;
Ojúmo Ire mó mi lónìí;
Mo níre gbogbo;
Màrìwò Òpè já sòòrò kanlè;
Ì wo má lawo ojúmó Ire.

Translation:
A new palm is straight from tip to base
He was the one who took Ifá for the citizens of the town of
ìlalà
Where the days of ire usually dawned
The day of ire had dawned for me today
I assure spouse
Màriwò Ọ'pẹ̀ já ṣòòrò kanlẹ̀
You are the Awo of the dawn of all the IRE
A day of ire dawns for me today
I give birth of children to children.
Màriwò Ọ'pẹ̀ já ṣòòrò kanlẹ̀
You are the Awo of the dawn of all the IRE
A day of ire dawns for me today
I assure all the ire of life
You are the awo of all the dawn of all ire
Ifá says that the client for whom this odu is revealed will
never experience sadness or disappointment in his life, you
must be very hard-working, patient and hopeful and all the
life will be yours.

Ifá says that with determination, hard work, patience and
prayers you will be able to obtain all the things in life, which
make people offer congratulations to those who obtain it,

wealth, a spouse, children, cars, etc. things, establish business, reputation, popularity, etc.

OGBE OGUNDA VERSE 2

Ení ti n bínú eni;
Níí taari nnkan eni sínú omi;
Èèyàn ti ò bínú;
Níí taari rè sókè;
Díá fún Mogbárímú;
Tíí se omo Òrìsa.

Translation:
Those who are envious of personality
It belongs to someone who kicks one's belongings into the river
Those who are not envious
They are the ones who kick them back to the surface of the earth
They were the ones who called and launched Ifá for Mogbárimú
Who was the offspring of Ọ̀rìṣà

PROPHESY

Ifá says that the Orí of the client for whom this odu is revealed will be his greatest support in his life, you will bear adversity through the assistance of your Orí, you will ensure abundant wealth and all the other will go through your Orí.

Ifá also says that while the adversary of the client for whom Ogbè-Ìyónú is revealed are busy plotting to harm, mutilate, kill you or cause you to experience loss. Your Orí will be directing those who will ensure that the plot is failing for you. Consequently, this client needs to offer sacrifice and perform rituals to Orí, Ifá and Ọbàtálá.

Pàtaki

Mogbárimú (I hold my head as a support) was the son of Ọbàtálá she went to the Awo mentioned above for the Ifá consultation. She wanted to know if she had any chance to become a successful woman in her life. in that case, what were the steps she would need to take in order to achieve this success.

She was assured that she was going to become a very successful woman in her life, she was also told that she would have many enemies but her Orí, Ifá and Ọbàtálá would help her overcome the opposition and she would achieve success. She was advised to offer sacrifice with two guinea fowl, two pigeons, palm oil and money. She was also asked to perform a ritual with her Orí with four kola nuts, four bitter kola, one white pigeon and a hen. Guinea. She had to perform the Ifá ritual with two rats, two fish and palm oil. She had to perform a ritual to Òrishànlá with native chalk, two snails (slug) and a white pigeon. She complied.

Since that time, whenever she thought to do something, her Orí, Ifá and Ọbàtálá clear the coast and ensure that she achieved her mission without much trouble. When in life those who were envious of her achievements planned any

31

evil, the three deities would ensure that other people who would foil such evil plans were equally available and the evil plans would not work. That was how Mogbárimú could easily understand her life ambition.

Ení ti n bínú eni;
Níí taari nnkan eni sínú omi;
Èèyàn ti ò bínú;
Níí taari rè sókè;
Díá fún Mogbárímú;
Tíí se omo Òrìsa. Wón ní kó sákáalè, ebo ní síse;
Ó gbé'bo, Ó rúbo;
Bí e bá í jí lówùúrò;
E di Èdá mú;
Orí eni làwúre eni.
Translation:
Those who are envious of personality
It belongs to someone who kicks one's belongings into the river
Those who are not envious
They are the ones who kick them back to the surface of the earth
They were the ones who called and launched Ifá for Mogbárimú
Who was the offspring of Òrìsà
they advised him to offer sacrifice
She complied.
If you wake up early in the morning
Hold your ORI (with both hands)
The ORI is a pathfinder to success.
Ifá dice que este cliente debe siempre estar sosteniendo su o su cabeza con su o sus dos manos y oraciones de la oferta a

su o su ORI para la ayuda. Ifá y Òrishànlá también ayuda al cliente, nadie puede impedirle al cliente tener éxito en la vida.

OGBE OGUNDA VERSE 3

A sá taara;
A rìn taara;
Òtààrà taara n'ìsàn odò;
Ojú odún méta lobìrin fi n jeun owó oko;
Díá fún Òrúnmìlà;
Baba yóó s'àsè bó ogbogbo Irúnmolè lórún;
Wón ní kó sákáalè, ebo ní síse;
Ó gbé'bo, Ó rúbo

Translation:
To run majestically
To make long and difficult trips majestically
Majestically and steadily are the torrents that flow
For three good years, a newly married wife consumes from her husband (without contributing financially)
They were the ones who project Ifá for Orunmila
Those who will celebrate or all Irunmolé in a time of five days
He was advised to offer sacrifice
He obeyed.

PROPHESY

Ifá says that the client who is revealed this odú is revealed for whom he will become a great leader on whom many people will depend. You will be feeding many people who will be under your direct command. You will be very wealthy and command authority. You need the good will of the people however before this can happen.

Pàtaki

Orunmila went with his students mentioned above to consult and determine the best way to gain respectability, honor, prestige, wealth and influence. Orunmila was informed that all this will be his but that he must request the good will of his colleagues, neighbors and those who wish him well. He was advised to have a party in which he would serve a variety of food.

He should also have variable drinks in such a way that all the guests would eat and drink to his satisfaction. At the end of the party, the guests would offer prayers to Orunmila and wish him well in his promises (or undertakings). This, however, must be done more than 5 days after the Ifá revelation. Orunmila was also asked to perform a ritual to Ifá with 2 rats and two fish, palm oil and money. He obeyed, all the guests arrived, celebrated to his satisfaction and expressed his goodwill to Orunmila.

Ifá says that his client will be very influential in his life. You must solicit goodwill and human support. You must give a party where many people will be invited to eat and drink, many people will depend on him or her for their livelihoods.

Orunmila went with his students mentioned above to consult and determine the best way to gain respectability, honor, prestige, wealth and influence. Orunmila was informed that all this will be his but that he must request the good will of his colleagues, neighbors and those who wish him well. He was advised to have a party in which he would serve a variety of food.

He should also have variable drinks in such a way that all the guests would eat and drink to his satisfaction. At the end of the party, the guests would offer prayers to Orunmila and wish him well in his promises (or undertakings), this, however, must be done more than five days after the Ifá revelation. Orunmila was also asked to perform a ritual to Ifá with two rats and two fish, palm oil and money. He obeyed, all the guests arrived, celebrated to his satisfaction and expressed his goodwill to Orunmila.

Ifá says that his client will be very influential in his life. You must solicit goodwill and human support. You must give a party where many people will be invited to eat and drink, many people will depend on him or her for their livelihoods.

A sá taara;
A rìn taara;
Òtààrà taara n'ìsàn odò;
Ojú odún méta lobìrin fi n jeun owó oko;
Díá fún Òrúnmìlà;
Ifá yóó s'àsè bó ogbogbo Irúnmolè lórún;
Wón ní kó sákáalè, ebo ní síse;
Ó gbé'bo, Ó rúbo;
Mo níyán;
Mo lòbè;
Oore ènìyàn ni mo wá gbà;

Mo lótí;
Mo lókà;
Oore ènìyàn ni mi wá gbà;
Oore ènìyàn.

Translation
To run majestically
To make long and difficult trips majestically
Majestically and steadily are the torrents that flow
For three good years, a newly married wife consumes from
her husband (without contributing financially)
They were the ones who project Ifá for Orunmila
Those who will celebrate or all Irunmolé in a time of five
days
He was advised to offer sacrifice
I will prepare mashed yam
I will prepare ground flour
It is the good will of the people that I come to acquire
I will prepare gin (prepared with palm wine)
I got wine (made with corn)
It is the goodwill of the people that I come to acquire the
goodwill of the people
Ifá says that this client will be able to achieve his life
ambitions from him. You, however, should never
overestimate the contributions of your colleagues, friends,
and well-wishers.

A sá taara;
A rìn taara;
Òtààrà taara n'ìsàn odò;
Ojú odún méta lobìrin fi n jeun owó oko;
Díá fún Òrúnmìlà;

36

Ifá yóó s'àsè bó ogbogbo Irúnmolè lórún;
Wón ní kó sákáalè, ebo ní síse;
Ó gbé'bo, Ó rúbo;
Mo níyán; Mo lòbè;
Oore ènìyàn ni mo wá gbà;
Mo lótí;
Mo lókà;
Oore ènìyàn ni mi wá gbà;
Oore ènìyàn.

Translation
To run majestically
To make long and difficult trips majestically
Majestically and steadily are the torrents that flow
For three good years, a newly married wife consumes from
her husband (without contributing financially)
They were the ones who project Ifá for Orunmila
Those who will celebrate or all Irunmolé in a time of five
days
He was advised to offer sacrifice
I will prepare mashed yam
I will prepare ground flour
It is the good will of the people that I come to acquire
I will prepare gin (prepared with palm wine)
I got wine (made with corn)
It is the goodwill of the people that I come to acquire the
goodwill of the people
Ifá says that this client will be able to achieve his life
ambitions from him. You, however, should never
overestimate the contributions of your colleagues, friends,
and well-wishers.

OGBE OGUNDA VERSO 4

Inú bíbí níí so ibi ti wón ti wá;
Alájàngbulà níí fiira rèé hàn;
O tún kó'seè rè dé, orúko níí so'ni;
Díá fún Òjòlá;
Díá fún Sèbé;
Díá fún Oká;
Díá fún Nìnì;
Tíí s'omo ìkeyìn-i won;
Tí yóó je Alápà-Níràwé;
Nílé Oníyanja;
Wón ní kó sákáalè, ebo ní síse

Translation.
Uncontrollable temper usually reveals his experience
He who fights without paying attention begs for a truce ends
Exposing himself (in bad light)
"you-have-come-again-with-your-attitude", will give only a (bad) name
They were the ones who project Ifá by Òjòlá (boa constrictor)
And they project the same for Sèbé (striped viper)
They also project for Oká (cobra)
And they project the same for Níní (a non-poisonous viper with a beautiful necklace)
who was the last to be born
When competing for the place of Alápà- Niràwé
In the land of Oniyanja
You are advised to offer sacrifice

PROPHESY

Ifá says that the client for whom this adú is revealed will be granted a title. Ifá says that the client will compete with many others to obtain a title, position or honor. Ifá says that the other contestants may be more qualified than him, academically, financially or socially, but you will take the position away from him. Ifá says, however, that the client must be patient and must be able to absorb insults, intimidation and provocations from people. These are the qualities that will give you the standing against all things weird.

Pàtaki

Alápà-Niràwé was the official title of the king of Àpá, when he was on the throne, the Estera community was very peaceful and prosperous. Everyone in the community was very happy. After reigning for several years, he was reunited with his ancestors. However, he gave birth to 4 children before his death. They were Òjòlá (boa constrictor), the eldest. He was followed by Sèbé (striped viper), after Sèbé was Oká (cobra) while the last was niní (a non-venomous viper with a beautiful color)

The council of those who make kings of the Àpá people was aware of the attitude of the first three sons who were evil, unforgivable and vindictive. Based on this, they invited the four children to consult with Ifá to determine who would be the next Àlapá-Niràwé from the town of Àpá.

The council of those who make kings also invited the three Awos mentioned above to consult Ifá. During the consultation, Ogbè-Ògúndán (Ogbe-Ìyònú) was revealed.

The Awos advised each of the four consultants to offer sacrifice with 2 chickens, 2 guinea fowl, palm oil and money, they were also advised to make sure to exercise a lot of patience, absorb insults, show magnanimity, never get angry when intimidated and make sure that they would never be provoked to anger. Only Níní obeyed the advice of the Awo and also offered the sacrifice.

Immediately they left, Òjòlá, Sèbé and Oká considered the advice of the Awo as a design to undermine their authority (theirs) and belittle them in the presence of their subjects. Anyone who crossed the path of Òjòlá was repressed (or swallowed). Sèbé used to bite anyone he saw. Anyone who stepped on Oka's tail was mercilessly bitten. Those who came through Níní were usually surprised to see how submissive, tolerant and gentle he was. They would immediately step on or kick him, but he would not retaliate.

A few months later, all the citizens of Àpá converged on the market and organized a meeting at the house of the director of those who make kings. They sang songs that the people preferred to have Níní as the next Àlapá-Niràwé. The director of those who make (elect) kings, organized a meeting with the council of those who make kings, invited the Awo to consult Ifá (Ogbe-Ìyònú) was revealed.

Ifá confirmed the appointment of Níní as the future of Òjòlá, Sèbé and Oká protested against the decision, but the entire community told them that they lost their opportunity as a result of their malevolent behavior.

Níní was so happy that he offered sacrifice again however he was told that he cannot offer the same sacrifice twice on the same subject in the same Odú. Then he was full of praise for the Awo who were in turn praising Órúnmìlá while Órúnmìlá was giving praise to Olòdùmarè:

Inú bíbí níí so ibi ti wón ti wá;
Alájàngbulà níí fiira rèé hàn;
O tún kó'seè rè dé, orúko níí so'ni;
Díá fún Òjòlá;
Díá fún Sèbé;
Díá fún Oká;
Díá fún Nìnì;
Tíí s'omo ìkeyìn-i won;
Tí yóó je Alápà-Níràwé;
Nílé Oníyanja;
Wón ní kó sákáalè, ebo ní síse;
Nìnì nìkan ní nbe léyìn, tó ntubo;
Lóoóto la mú Nìnì joba;
Òjòlá ló sìwà hù;
Ló ba ìsee rè jé;
Lóoóto la mú Nìnì joba;
Sèbé ló sìwà hù;
Ló ba ìsee rè jé;
Lóoóto la mú Nìnì joba;
Lóoóto la mú Nìnì joba;
Oká ló sìwà hù;

41

Ló ba ìsee rè jé;
Lóoóto la mú Nìnì joba
Translation.
Uncontrollable temper usually reveals his experience
He who fights without paying attention begs for a truce end
Exposing himself (in bad light)
"You-have-come-again-with-your-attitude", will give only a (bad) name
They were the ones who project Ifá by Òjòlá (boa constrictor)
And they project the same for Sèbé (striped viper)
They also project for Oká (cobra)
And they project the same for Níní (a non-poisonous viper with a beautiful necklace)
who was the last to be born
When competing for the place of Alápà- Niràwé
In the land of Oniyanja
You are advised to offer sacrifice
Only Níní heeded his advice.
Truly we, we gave throne to Níní
Òjòlá was the one who misbehaved
And I spoil your destiny
Verily, we gave throne to Níní
Verily, we gave throne to Níní
Sèbé was the one who misbehaved
And I spoil your destiny
Verily, we gave throne to Níní
Verily, we gave throne to Níní
Oká was the one who had bad behavior
And I spoil your destiny
Verily, we gave throne to Níní
Ifá says that this prevents Ire from a prestigious title, for the

person for whom Ogbe-Ìyònú is revealed. Ifá says that you will get the title through patience, kindness and ability to control your temper in the face of opposition, oppression, provocation or intimidation of rights. You will become a leader of the people. You too will become the people's choice.

OGBE OGUNDA VERSE 5

Inú bíbí Ò dá nnkan;
Sùúrù ni baba iwà;
Àgbà tó ní sùúrù;
Ohun gbogbo ló ní;
Díá fún Òrúnmìlà;
Baba n lo rèé fé Ìyà;
Tíí se omo Oníwòó;
Wón ní kó sákáalè, ebo ní síse;
Ó gbé'bo, Ó rúbo

Translation:
Anger adds to nothing fruitful
Patience is the father of (good) character
The superior owns everything
These were the declarations of the Oracle of Orunmila
When he went to look for the hand of the Ìyà (suffering)
The daughter of Oníwòò (King of Ìwò)
They advised him to offer sacrifice
He complied.

PROPHESY

Ifá says that he foresees the Ire of a good wife for the client for whom Ogbe-Ìyònú is revealed. Ifá says that the lady in question is the daughter of an important personality in society.

Ifá says that the client can be patient and he should not allow himself to be provoked into anger. Ifá also says that the parents of the lady in question will put many tests for him. The entire test is animated by her determining her level of patience, testing her willpower and ensuring that he was patient enough to be a loving husband and take care of her. Ifá says that, with patience, he will be able to win the test.

Pàtaki

Ìyà was the daughter of Oníwòò of Ìwò. She was good looking and very hardworking.

She was also loved by Oníwòò. Therefore, Oníwòò resolved to take active in the mate option of him. Oníwòò wanted to make sure that anyone who will marry his beloved daughter must be patient and not easily provoked. He set different tests accordingly for the likely applicants. All of them failed.

Orunmila then went to some of these students to consult Ifá and determine whether or not he would marry Ìyà the daughter of Oníwòó. he also wanted to know if the relationship would be fruitful and happy for both of them. The students assured him of the relationship that it would be very rewarding for him if he entered into it. He was advised however that he be very patient and should not be provoked. He was informed that Ìyà's parents will put much

44

to the test for him to determine her patience and the level of her patience. They then advised him to offer sacrifice with a rooster. Palm oil and money. (For the client, he or she also needs to perform an Ifá ritual with two rats, fish and money). He complied and left on his journey.

When Orunmila arrived at Oníwòó's palace, he was warmly received and asked for a room to sleep. Unknown to Orunmila, the room was an Oníwòó pig sty. Above it was where the Oniwòó chickens were kept. For three days, Orunmila was kept inside this room without food or water. The room stank intolerably and the chickens defecated onto Orunmila's body. He never went out, he never begged for food, and he never asked for water to cleanse his body.

On the fourth day, Oníwòó summoned Orunmila to his palace, when he saw him, he was full of eses and he was stinking terribly. He asked Orunmila if he had enjoyed his stay in his room. Orunmila replied that the room was like a second palace for him. Orunmila was asked to go to another room next to the kitchen so the heat and smoke were suffocating him. He stayed inside the room for another three days without food or drink. On the fourth day, he summoned the palace to the presence of Oníwòó. He asked Orunmila if he would have enjoyed his stay in his room. Orunmila replied that the room was very nice. Oníwòó asked that Orunmila should be given food, for the first time. He ate the food.

The next room given to him was full of stale water, worms

45

and insects. He couldn't sleep for the three days he spent inside the room. They asked him to leave the room. He had insect bites all over his body. When Oníwòó asked him if he had enjoyed his stay in the room, Orunmila answered affirmatively.

For three months, Orunmila was going from one test to another. He endured everything without complaining. The next three months were physical tests, such as cutting down large trees at registration time, clearing large tracts of land, and carrying heavy loads from one place to another. All these he did without complaint.

After this, Oníwòó summoned Orunmila, to meet him go and take his bath. She changed into a new dress, presented to him by Oníwòó. Before he went back to the palace court, he found it everywhere and we were all in a festive mood. We were all singing, dancing and partying. Oníwòó asked Orunmila to sit besides him, he did. Oníwòó gave up Ìyà then for him to take home as his wife. Oníwòó praised Orunmila's patience, patience and meek clinging throughout his trials. He then asked Orunmila to take care of Ìyà for him, since he had shown that he was capable of taking good care of a woman.

Orunmila was full of joy, that he had succeeded in the future, where some others had failed. He then said that day, with lit pupils, that all women to marry in a man's house, or those who married on the arm of a man, should be called Ìyà-Ìwo or Ìyàwò (the suffering to the Ìwò). He then called his new wife Èrè Ìyà-Ìwo (profit for his suffering in the town of the Ìwò). Everyone, him and also his director. From that day on, all wives were known as Ìyàwò.

Inú bíbí Ò dá nnkan;
Sùúrù ni baba iwà;
Àgbà tó ní sùúrù;
Ohun gbogbo ló ní;
Díá fún Òrúnmìlà;
Baba n lo rèé fé Ìyà;
Tíí se omo Oníwòó;
Wón ní kó sákáalè, ebo ní síse;
Ó gbé'bo, Ó rúbo;
Kò pé, kó jìnnà;
E wá bá wa ní wòwó Ireti Òrúnmìlà je ní Ìwó;
Kó seé dele wí; E wá wo Ìyà-Ìwó!

Translation:
Anger adds to nothing fruitful
Patience is the father of (good) character
The superior owns everything
These were the declarations of the Oracle of Orunmila
When he went to look for the hand of the Ìyà (suffering)
The daughter of Oníwòò (King of Ìwò)
They advised him to offer sacrifice
He complied.
Before long, not too far
Meet us in the midst of all the anger
The suffering that Orunmila experienced at the Ìwó
Not worth it
Look at my Ìyà-Ìwó (the award of suffering to the Ìwó)
Ifá says that the client is following something very important

47

to his life from you. Ifá says that the thing, if insured, will change the client's life for the better. You must offer sacrifice, be patient and be ready to endure suffering and undue provocation to follow him. The such thing can be a job, a position, a business contract, a promotion, and so on. The end will more than compensate for the sufferings experienced before achieving the goal.

OGBE OGUNDA VERSE 6

Ó tán, o kún o;
O d'ìgbà ó se o;
Díá fún Òdèdè;
Ó nlo soko Iyàrá dalé-dalé;
Díá fún Yàrá, Ó nlo saya Òdèdè dale-dale.

Translation:
Hi, how are you?
Long time ago
They were the ones who projected Ifá for Ôdèlè (living room)
While planning to marry Iyàrá (ward) until old age
They also project Ifá for Iyàrá
While she will become Ôdèlè's wife for life

PROPHESY

Ifá says that she anticipates the IRE of the good wife for the male client and the Ire of the good husband for the female client for whom this odú is revealed. Ifá says that their relationship with them has been sanctioned from heaven

48

and no one would be able to separate them.

Ifá says that many people will oppose their relationship, but there is nothing anyone can do, since the relationship enjoys divine approval.

Pàtaki

Ôdèlè and Iyàrá (living room and room) were lovers for a long time. They had become virtually inseparable. The relationship was, however, being opposed by some people because they were trained on the same compound and by the same person. Consequently, they went to the Awo mentioned above to determine the chances of their relationship resisting opposition and flourishing in marriage.

He was advised to offer sacrifice with two guinea fowl and 2 roosters, palm oil and money, while the woman was asked to offer sacrifice with two guinea fowl, two hens, palm oil and money. They both obeyed. They were advised to ignore all opposition and go ahead with their wedding plans.

They started planning their wedding. Soon, those who opposed the marriage went to register their displeasure, but were rebuffed.

Both Ôdèlè and Iyàrá lived happily ever after, they were also blessed with many children, until today, Ôdèlè is still married to Iyàrá.

Ó tán, o kún o;
O d'ìgbà ó se o;

Díá fún Òdèdè;
Ó nlo soko Iyàrá dalé-dalé;
Díá fún Yàrá, Ó nlo saya Òdèdè dale-dale;
Wón ní kó sákáalè, ebo ní síse;
Ó gbé'bo, Ó rúbo;
Èyín ò gbón o;
Èyín ò mòràn;
Èyín ò mò wìpé Òdèdè n soko Iyàrá lo o.
Translation
Hi, how are you?
Long time ago
They were the ones who projected Ifá for Ôdèlè (living
room)
While planning to marry Iyàrá (ward) until old age
They also project Ifá for Iyàrá
While she will become Ôdèlè's wife for life
They were advised to offer sacrifice
they obeyed
you are not wise at all
You also lack deep knowledge
You cannot know that Ôdèlè is Iyàrá's husband for life.
Ifá says that it anticipates the IRE of realization passes two
people for whom Ogbe-Ìyònú is revealed. Ifá says that both
will achieve success despite the opposition of many in the
neighborhood.

OGBE OGUNDA VERSE 7

Àkúé kandé;
Ègàn Ìwémè;
Àkúé Ìwémè kandé-ko;
Díá fún Àgàràwú;
Tó n sukún;

mo ròde Èègùn;
Wón ní kó sákáalè, ebo ní síse;
Ó gbé'bo, Ó rúbo
Translation:
forty units of money
What is the sack of money of the Iwémè people
The money of the people of Iwémè is in quarantine and
twenty
They were the ones who projected for Àgaráwú
While they cried to the community of Èègùn for their lack
of children
She was advised to offer sacrifice
she obeyed

PROPHESY

Ifá says that she prevents the ire of many children for the
client for whom Ogbè-Ògúndá is revealed. Ifá says that he
or she will give birth to many children, if the client is
suffering from childlessness, as soon as the appropriate
sacrifice is made, he or she will have many children. In effect,
the client will have children until he or she is tired of having
more children.

Pàtaki

Àgaráwú was a native of Iwémè, a town in the Republic of
Benin. She belonged to the (speaking) tribe of Èègùn. She
was married for a long time without any facts or news. She
then approached the awo mentioned above who were also
Èègùn by tribe. She left her dwelling place in the Yoruba

51

land and cried to Iwémè her town to meet the Babalawo.

They advised him to offer sacrifice with four hens and a lot of money. She was also asked to find a hoe and saber that are not in use. She obeyed. The Babalawo in turn made a large Òkìtì (heap or pile) and put the Hoe and the saber there. They offered sacrifice for Àgaráwú and propitiated the Òkìtì.

Soon, her womb split open and she had many children. She was dancing and singing praises to her awo.

Àkúé kandé;
Ègàn Ìwémè;
Àkúé Ìwémè kandé-ko;
Díá fún Àgàràwú;
Tó n sukún omo ròde Èègùn;
Wón ní kó sákáalè, ebo ní síse;
Ó gbé'bo, Ó rúbo;
Kò pé, kó jìnnà;
Ire omo wá ya dé tùtúre;
Àgàràwú wáa dolómo;
E wá womo Èègùn beere.

Translation
forty units of money
What is the sack of money of the Iwémè people
The money of the people of Iwémè is in quarantine and twenty
They were the ones who projected for Àgaráwú
While they cried to the community of Èègùn for their lack of children

52

She was advised to offer sacrifice
she obeyed
Before time, not too far
Find us in the center of many children
Àgaráwú now becomes a proud mother of children
Come and see the children of Èègùn in multitude.
Ifá says that this client will have many children. There will be so many that he or she will decide when to stop having children of their own.

OGBE OGUNDA VERSE 8

Ògbólógbòó Babaláwo, abìróké jìngbìnnì-jìgbinni;
Díá fún Ìyálé Olóbà;
Ó nmójú ekún sùngbérè omo;
Wón ní kó sákáalè, ebo ní síse;
Ó gbé'bo, Ó rúbo

Translation
An old Babaláwo with his great experience and his old oily candle
He was the one who launched Ifá as the oldest wife
When she was crying in lamentation for not having children
She was advised to offer a sacrifice.
She complied.

PROPHESY

Ifá says that the ire provides a sterile woman with a child for whom Ogbe-Ìyònú is revealed. Ifá says that when a child has arrived, he should be called Omọwùmí – I prefer a child.

Pàtaki

Iyálé Olóba was the oldest wife of King Oba. She was barren all the wives married after having given birth to many children, all these wives had tested Iyálé Olóba. She had never given birth to any children, they added, that she could only be useful in caring for her wives' children. For this reason, the wives left, they could leave their children in the care of Iyálé Olóba.

Initially, she didn't think about any of this. But when she found out that this was being done on purpose to look down on her, she became sad and wept bitterly. Consequently, she went to the aforementioned old Babalawo for Ifá consultation.

The Babalawo assured her that her womb would open. She was advised to offer a sacrifice with her best dress, a wrapper, and a blouse. After getting the dress, she would say that, "I prefer a boy because of this dress", she was also asked to prepare a soup with a lot of meat, vegetables and ewedu. Everything was cooked in a large pot and part of it was used to perform rituals to her Ègbè de ella. She complied with what was dictated by the Babalawo.

After a while her heavenly gaze assured him that her womb would open to give birth. She became pregnant and gave birth to a baby. She called him Omówùmí meaning "I prefer a boy".

Ògbólógbòó Babaláwo, abìróké jìngbìnnì-jigbinni;
Díá fún Ìyálé Olóbà;
Ó nmójú ekún sùngbérè omo;
Wón ní kó sákáalè, ebo ní síse;
Ó gbé'bo, Ó rúbo;
Kò pé, kó jìnnà;
Ire omo wá ya dé tùtúru;
Omo wá wù mí j'aso ló o;
E wá wo Ìyálé Olóbà;
Omo wù mí ò, j'aso lo o.

Translation:
An old Babalawo with his great experience and his old oily candle
He was the one who launched Ifá as the oldest wife
When she was crying in lamentation for not having children
She was advised to offer a sacrifice.
She complied.
After a while, not very long
The ire of birth come abundantly
however, I prefer a child to dresses
Look at the oldest wife of Olóbà
I prefer a child to dresses
Ifá says that the client, which Ogbe-Ìyònú was revealed to him, will be able to fulfill the desires of her heart. You need to offer a sacrifice and propitiate her Ẹgbẹ̀ as described before.

OGBE OGUNDA VERSE

Arúgbó odó la fi n gún èlú;
Àgbàlagbà ònà níí g'éjò méjì gberegede;
Díá fún Baba tí n tún ilé onílé se;

Èyí tí Àjàgùnmàlè yóó maa wolé dè;

Wón ní kó sákáalè, ebo ní síse;

Ó gbé'bo, Ó rúbo.

Translation:

Only an old and worn mortar is used to dress indigo

An old and constantly used place is what divides the snake in two

They invoke Ifá for the old man who brings peace to people's homes

Those whose house will be venerated by the heavenly priest

He was asked to offer sacrifice.

He did it.

PROPHESY

Ifá says to foresee the ire of happiness for a male/male client to whom this odu was revealed. Ifá says that the client must be initiated in Ifá and he must be / be practicing as Babalawo.

Ifá says that many people would abuse him in his career projection, but he should ignore them because all those who abuse him will return to reward him and seek favor from him.

Pàtaki

Baba-Onírú-Ire (a god who fears man) went to the place mentioned before to consult Ifá, he wanted to know what he needed to become a successful man and it was suggested to him to go with Ifá for his initiation and start his study.

56

They told him that he was destined to be a Babalawo from heaven. He was asked to focus on healing and bringing peace and joy into people's lives. The Babalawo asked him to bring a goat, 16 pigeons, 16 birds (8 roosters and 8 hens). 16 rats, 16 fish, and initiation money.

He fulfilled everything.

Immediately he began to study Ifá as a profession, criticism began to pour in from his immediate family, they called him by various degrading names. His wife and children threatened to abandon him if he continued with his Ifá education.

He ignored them all and pursued his chosen career with renewed vigor.

Five years later, he completed his studies and wherever he went, he healed the sick, gave hope to those whose cases seemed hopeless, patience to those who had too much anxiety to achieve and longing within his heart. Everyone who came in contact with him only showed praise towards him, because everyone had a reason to rejoice.

Back at his house, Àjàgùnmàlè made sure that all the financial, social, and emotional needs of his family were met, by all those who had come to show them his gratitude. Soon even those, who had vehemently opposed his choice of Ifá career, joined him in praising him. He and his family were happy and satisfied. He was singing, dancing and praising Olódúmarè, for having made him a successful and happy man, in his chosen career. He also praised Olódúmarè, for having given him strength to resist the initial opposition of the people from him.

Aturuku odó la fi n gún èlú;
Àgbàlagbà ònà níí g'éjò méjì gberegede;
Díá fún Baba tí n tún ilé onílé se;
Èyí tí Àjàgùnmàlè yóó maa wolé dè;
Wón ní kó sákáalè, ebo ní síse;
Ó gbé'bo, Ó rúbo;
Baba n bú mi l'óle;
Ìyá n bú mi l'óle;
Aya ti mo fé n bú mi l'óle;
Omo ti mo bí n bú mi l'óle;
Òrò ò kàn yìn o;
Lówó Elédáà mi mi o;
Àse wá dowó Ogbè òhun Ògúndá.

Translation
Only an old and worn mortar is used to dress indigo
An old and constantly used place is what divides the snake in two
They invoke Ifá for the old man who brings peace to people's homes
Those whose house will be venerated by the heavenly priest
He was asked to offer sacrifice.
He did it.
He replied: my father says that I am a lazy man
My mother abuses and calls me lazy
My wife abuses and calls me lazy
My children abuse and call me lazy
It's none of your business
It's for your destiny

58

I delegate my authority to Ogbe and Ògúndá.
Ifá says that I will never put the client from whom this odú
is revealed to shame if he follows the path laid out for him
by Ifá. Ifá says that all those who have made bad gestures
towards him will later praise him.

OGBE OGUNDA VERSE 10

Inú bíbí ni ò da nnkan fún'ni;
Sùúrù ni baba ìwà;
Àgbà tó ní sùúrù;
A j'ogbó; A j'ató;
A j'ayé Ifá rindin-rindin bí eni nlá'yin;
Díá fún Orí Inú;
A bù fún tí ìta o;
Wón ní kó sákáalè, ebo ní síse

Translation:
Uncontrollable temper amounts to nothing for human
beings
Patience is the father of all people
An older man who is patient
As much as older must follow
he will grow a lot
He will enjoy the life of Ifá as someone enjoying the honeys
Those were the declarations of the oracle for Orí-Òde
(destiny)
The two of them were foreshadowed to offer sacrifice.

PROPHESY

Ifá says that the client for whom this odu is revealed should
never be disturbed, he or she must show patience at all

59

times, Ifá says that the client has a very good destiny, but no matter how good a destiny he may have, a bad temper can come out if your opportunities to actualize your potentialities and capacities in life.

Pàtaki

Orí-Inú and Orí-Òde were inseparable companions. Both influenced human life and its advancements on Earth. Fate thought that they were not important to humans, the characters (beings) consequently, fate refused to recognize the importance of beings. Those who were destined to be rich became poor because of their bad people. Those who were destined to be kings were slaves, because of their bad characters (personality), those who were destined to be leaders, were followers of those who were less qualified than them because of their bad personality. This led to destiny to take advantage of the Babalawo mentioned above, to consult Ifá.

The Awo then pronounced the declaration of the Ifá Oracle to Orí and asked Orí to offer sacrifice with two roosters, two pigeons and a monkey or monkey. Orí was also called to propitiate Orí-Inú. Orí was going to have the Dúndún leaves and tẹ̀tẹ̀ leaves, corn and money. He completed with the guidelines of the Awo. The maize was dissolved in water together with the Dúndún and tẹ̀tẹ̀ leaves and the fat, spread on the shell and added to the mixture. Ìyẹ̀ròsún was later used to mark Ogbe-Ìyọ̀nú on the divination board and this stanza was placed on it. Everything got mixed up. Ori was called to drink the concoction. He did it and they used it to smear it on his ship while saying: My personality, I recognize the importance of him. Please don't spit out my fate. Later the concoction was returned to Èsù shrine.

After doing all this, the Babalawo told Orí (destiny) never stop estimating the importance of Orí-Inú. He said that personality in life was as important as destiny. A person can have the best destiny, but if he does not match the personality, the destiny will not be complete. On the other hand, if another person has bad destiny and good personality, this will improve his destiny and good personality, this will improve his destiny. A person may not be a very successful man in his daily life.

From then on, Orí agreed to recognize Orí-Inú and thus achieve great advances. Those who will fail or refuse to give Orí-Inú recognition of him at his own risk.

Inú bíbí ni ò da nnkan fún'ni;
Sùúrù ni baba ìwà;
Àgbà tó ní sùúrù;
A j'ogbó;
A j'ató;
A j'ayé Ifá rindin-rindin bí eni nlá'yin;
Díá fún Orí Inú;
A bù fún tí ìta o;
Wón ní kó sákáalè, ebo ní síse;
Ó gbé'bo, Ó rúbo;
Àpárí inú me, ejó re jààre;
Má ba t'òde mi jé.

Translation:

Uncontrollable temper amounts to nothing for human beings

Patience is the father of all people

An older man who is patient

As much as older must follow

he will grow a lot

He will enjoy the life of Ifá as someone enjoying the honeys

Those were the declarations of the oracle for Orí-Òde (destiny)

The two of them were foreshadowed to offer sacrifice.

they sacrificed

My personality I recognize my importance please do not spit my destiny.

Ifá says that the client must have good habits to reach the possibility of improving his potential as his destiny.

OGBE OGUNDA VERSE 11

Ìbínú kò da nnkan fún ni;

Sùúrù ni baba ìwà;

Àgbà tó ní sùúrù;

A j'ogbó;

A j'ató;

A j'ayé Ifá rindin-rindin bí eni nlá'yin;

Díá fún Èjè;

Ó nbá omo tuntún bò wáyé láti òrun;

Día fún Ekún;

Ó nbá omo tuntún bò wáyé láti òrun;

Día fún Èkín;

Ó nbá omo tuntún bò wáyé láti òrun;

Día fún sùúrù; Ó

nbá omo tuntún bò wáyé láti òrun;

Wón ní kó sákáalè, ebo ní síse
Translation:
Uncontrollable amounts of temperance for nothing by
human beings
Patience is the father of all character
the old man is patient
As the old will last longer
he will grow old
He will enjoy the life of Ifá as someone sucking honey
Those were declarations of the oracle to the blood
When they accompanied a newborn baby to the world from
the sky
The oracle declared the same thing to which he cried
When they accompanied a newborn baby to the world from
the sky
They also declared the one who laughed
When they accompanied a newborn baby to the world from
the sky
They spoke the same way to patience
When they accompanied a newborn baby to the world from
the sky
They were both suggested to offer sacrifices

PROPHESY

Ifá says that the Iré of prestige, honor and recognition for
the client, for whom this odú is revealed, is predictable. Ifá
says that many people were involved in this, Ifá says that
each one of them went to offer two different sacrifices for
prestige, honor and recognition, now also for the same in
the future.

Pàtaki

In heaven a newborn was about to descend into the world blood, crying, laughter, patience planned to accompany the unborn baby into the world. The four of them then proceeded to the house of baba that Ifá had mentioned to consult. They wanted to know if his journey into the world with the baby could be fruitful and rewarding for them. The Awo assured them that they would all be honored, respected and recognized in the world. They were advised to offer sacrifices that they could honor and respect immediately upon arrival on Earth. They would also offer another sacrifice so that respect and honor would be given to them on the first day they arrived on Earth and would last forever. They would offer a rooster and a hen; it is this first sacrifice (thus they would obtain honor and respect immediately upon arrival on Earth) and a pigeon and a guinea fowl so that the honor and respect will endure.

Only blood and tears offered the sacrifice for them, it would be agreed by honor and respect immediately when they arrive on Earth, while none of them will bother to offer the other sacrifice. Blood brought the sacrificial material first, after the sacrifice, blood was blessed that, without it, no human race could ever have seeds. They also blessed that blood would always herald the arrival of a new baby.

The spirits sanctioned the blessing and chanted Ase (so be it).

Llorto brought his own materials, after the sacrifice he was blessed that he will no longer cry. The fruit of human beings would not be useful to them, the heavenly spirits sanctioned the blessing. As laughter and patience, they did not offer any sacrifice, they were not blessed and also, they did not have the opportunity to accompany the baby that was going to be born.

The truth of the blessing of the Awo blood, announced the arrival of the new baby when the mother of several, went to childbirth, first saw blood, immediately the expectation of all around her was seen, it was high because the baby was about to be born, everyone was waiting for the arrival of the baby into the world, immediately after the baby came into the world, he began to cry and then those around him heard the baby's cry. Everyone began to sing and dance, congratulating the parents, saying prayers to Olòdúmarè. They said "a gbọ òhun iya, a gbọ òhun omọ" which meant that we heard the mother's voice in the baby's voice after the blessings of the Awos, that without crying the fruit of human beings would not be useful. It became true that if the child did not cry immediately after being born into the world, it could be spanked for shock therapy and if after that, it still did not cry, the baby would be assumed to be dead and no one would be happy if the baby did not cry. cries.

In addition to that, if a woman did not begin to see blood in the form of menstruation, she would not produce any fruit, if a newborn felt uncomfortable, it was through crying that one could begin to guess that it did, for example: if the baby was hungry, hot, cold, malaria, fever or others, only crying was revealed, without crying no one could guess.

Consequently, human beings depend on blood and crying in the execution of two functions, for which both sacrifices were offered. As honor, respect and recognition were agreed upon immediately upon reaching the world, but since they did not offer sacrifice for honor, respect and recognition, to last forever, their meaning would not go beyond that stage, meanwhile, on the fortieth day of the birth of the baby laughter, having noticed the kind of honor and respect and recognition that was accorded by blood and tears, he decided to return to the Awo's house, to offer his own sacrifice, he was told to offer, two roosters and two hens against each one of blood and crying they offered. Thus, honor and respect were accorded immediately upon arrival on Earth and he offered two pigeons and two guinea fowl. For honor and respect to be with him always. This time he complied.

After sacrifice, Risa was blessed as long as he was on Earth, he could be found where people were happy, where people had achieved great success, where anything good was happening to people, to many or to everyone. Risa then came into the world to meet the newborn after the fortieth day, the parents noticed that the baby began to smile. Later the baby started giggling and then laughing.

After seven out of nine months, Patience went to the Awos

to offer his own sacrifice, when he realized that the other three had already settled on Earth. The Babaláwo asked him to offer five roosters and five hens to reach an agreement of honor and respect that will last forever, patience offered the requested sacrifice.

By then the baby was already beginning to learn to walk, the baby in his haste to learn to walk fell, the parents warned him to be patient, after he mastered how to walk, he began to run and fell. His parents warned him to be patient in everything the baby wanted to do, patience became dominant in the baby's life, he had patience in walking, eating, running, talking, jumping, playing, dancing, singing, fighting and in other things.

The more the baby grew the more dominant were laughter and patience, on the other hand, the more the baby grew, the less desired blood and tears became, this was because only laughter and patience offered both sacrifices with honor, respect and recognition so that these attributes will last forever, blood and tears offered the first sacrifice, but refused to offer the second.

Since that day, all human beings prayed for them not to go to heaven with the same meanings with which they came to the world, that is, again with blood and tears, the prayers were for them to return to heaven with laughter and patience.

Ifá says that to provide eternal respect, honor and

recognition for the client for whom Ogbè-Ìyònú is revealed. Ifá strongly recommends for the client to offer the sacrifice for you to achieve these attributes now and another for you, to have all the attributes forever.

Laughter and patience he was singing and dancing and praising his Awo, who in turn was praising Órúnmìlá. Órúnmìlá was also praising Olódùmarè for this achievement.

Ìbínú kò da nnkan fún ni;
Sùúrù ni baba ìwà;
Àgbà tó ní sùúrù;
A j'ogbó;
A j'ató;
A j'ayé Ifá rindin-rindin bí eni nlá'yin;
Díá fún Èjè;
Ó nbá omo tuntún bò wáyé láti òrun;
Día fún Ekún;
Ó nbá omo tuntún bò wáyé láti òrun;
Día fún Èkín;
Ó nbá omo tuntún bò wáyé láti òrun;
Día fún sùúrù;
Ó nbá omo tuntún bò wáyé láti òrun;
Wón ní kó sákáalè, ebo ní síse;
Ó gbé'bo, Ó rúbo;
Kò pé, kó jìnnà;
E wá bá ni ní jèbútú Ire gbogbo
Translation:
Uncontrollable amounts of temperance for nothing by human beings
Patience is the father of all character

68

the old man is patient
As the old will last longer
he will grow old
He will enjoy the life of Ifá as someone sucking honey
Those were declarations of the oracle to the blood
When they accompanied a newborn baby to the world from the sky
The oracle declared the same thing to which he cried
When they accompanied a newborn baby to the world from the sky
They also declared the one who laughed
When they accompanied a newborn baby to the world from the sky
They spoke the same way to patience
When they accompanied a newborn baby to the world from the sky
They were both suggested to offer sacrifices
they fulfilled
Before long, not too far
Find us in the midst of abundant Ire.
Ifá says that, if someone has achieved or acquired something that brought happiness and laughter such an achievement, he was accompanied by patience, consequently, the client must be very patient in what he does, to achieve success in life.

Because blood and tears offered one sacrifice and refused to offer the other, they were initially called to herald life, but later to herald disaster and sorrow on the other hand, laughter and patience are always called to bring success, happiness and satisfaction.

OGBE OGUNDA VERSE 12

Òpópó t'ìrópó;
Òpòpò t'ìròpò;
Ò fi sééré kan dùùrù;
Ò fi dùùrù kan sééré;
Díá fún Òrúnmìlà;
Yóó se ooree kan ti kò níí mo ìdíi rè;
Wón ní kó sákáalè, ebo ní síse;
Ó gbé'bo, Ó rúbo.

Translation:
Òpópo t'irópó1
Òpópo t'irópó2
He who uses gourd of ṣẹ̀ẹ̀rẹ̀3 to hit musical instrument of dùùrù4
He who uses musical instrument of dùùrù to hit gourd of ṣẹ̀ẹ̀rẹ̀
They were the ones who launched Ifá for Ọ'rùnmilá
Who will do a great favor that he would not be aware of
They advised him to offer sacrifice
he fulfilled

PROPHESY

Ifá says that he foresees the iré of wealth, children and long life for the client for whom this odú is revealed. Ifá says that the client must exercise a lot of patience and all the good things in life will be for you.

Ifá says that the client should never engage in the practice of skipping meals. You should never abstain from food in the

70

form of fasting or dieting.

Ifá also says that, if an ailment is afflicting the client, or one of your intimate relationships. The affected person must have relief if he makes the appropriate sacrifice.

Ifá also says that this client will do an important person a favor. People will reciprocate the good deed. Therefore, the client must not show greed or must think of an immediate reward, something that you do for others.

Pàtaki

In heaven, Igún (vulture) was acting as the child of Olódúmarè. One day, Igún fell ill. He was weak, lean and fragile-seeming. He went to Olòdúmarè to complain about his state of health.

Olódúmarè asked Igún to proceed in the world and that he would find a remedy for his food on Earth. In light of this, Igun descended into the world.

On the other hand, Ọ̀rùnmilá was in his home. He had two wives who lived with him. He was poor and neither of the wives had handed over any problems to him. It was very difficult for Ọ̀rùnmilá to eat once for a day. He and his two wives did not have any good clothes that they could wear. They had no good accommodation to live in. Everything was very hard for them on Earth. He therefore called the students of his mentioned above, for the Ifá consultation. What steps did he need to be a successful person in life?

What should he do, for his two wives to get pregnant and give birth to children?

Órúnmìlá was sure that he would become a very successful man and that his wives would give birth to children in due course. He was informed that he was going to do a great favor for a very important person, of which he would not be aware. They told him further, that the person would pay many for the good deeds that Órúnmìlá did over him.

Órúnmìlá was advised to offer sacrifice with five hens, five bottles of palm oil and five new containers, then he would offer one of the hens to Ifá each day, for five days as a ritual. All the internal organs of each of the chickens, intestines, liver, gizzard and internal eggs would be removed, put inside a container, pour a bottle of palm oil into it and it would be taken to the shrine of Èsù Òdará, that would be offered each day for the five days. Órúnmìlá complied and did when he was advised.

Meanwhile, when Igún arrived on Earth, he landed near the tree where Órúnmìlá had deposited the compound. He found the sacrifice that Órúnmìlá had simply put there. Èsù Òdará persuaded Igún to eat the sacrifice. Igun did so and found that this stomach problem suddenly disappeared. The next day, Órúnmìlá repeated the sacrifice. Igun ate it and realized that the weakness in his right leg disappeared as well. On the third day, he ate the sacrifice offered by Órúnmìlá, he was fed and the problem in his right front limb disappeared. On the fourth day, he fed and the problem in his left leg disappeared. On the fifth day, he ate the sacrifice and the food in his left forelimb disappeared. Igun became totally fine on the fifth day. It was then that he understood that his illness was caused by lack of food. Igún then asked Èsù Òdará for the identity of the person who had fed him for five days. Èsù informed Igún that he was Órúnmìlá.

The next day Igún returned to heaven and informed Olódúmarè that he was perfectly fine and that it was through the food provided by Órúnmìlá that he recovered. Olódúmarè then told Igún that it was not good for Igún to deny himself. He shouldn't skip any meal again. Igun agreed.

Igún then told Olódúmarè that he (Igún) would like to repay Órúnmìlá for the good he had done for him.

Olódúmarè gave Igún four gifts – wealth – children – longevity – patience- to give to Órúnmìlá, so that he chooses one. Olódúmarè told Órúnmìlá he should not choose more than one of these gifts and that Igún should return with the rest to heaven.

Igún returned to Earth and went straight to Órúnmìlá's house with the four gifts. He thanked Órúnmìlá for the favor he had done for him. That was the first time that Órúnmìlá would know that the sacrifice he offered was responsible for making Igún recover his health, after many thanks. Igún told Órúnmìlá that he (Igún), had returned to pay him for his good deeds or deeds and that he, Órúnmìlá, was going to choose only one of the gifts as Olòdùmarè told

73

him.

Orunmila invited her two wives to deliberate, he asked the young wife what she felt she should choose from wealth, children, longevity and patience and the reason why they would prefer her.

The young wife chose wealth, when asked why, she replied that if they chose wealth, they would have enough resources to buy good clothes, good furniture and the latest materials from the town. She also claimed that it would be easy for them to build a new house, buy a new horse and be able to eat and drink whatever they wanted at any time.

The older wife was asked to choose one of the four gifts and give reasons for her choice. The older wife chose children. She said that, if children were chosen, she would be counted among those who had given birth to children in her life. She said that when she died, someone would give her a holy burial. For her that was more valuable than any other thing or action in life.

Òrúnmìlà invited her friend to advise him what to choose. The friend advised longevity. He would be able to live much longer than any other person in life. He would be able to tell stories that no other person could tell. He would be the most respected person for his age.

Òrúnmìlà then called her students to consult Ifá for the second time. During the consultation, Ogbe-Ìyònú was revealed. The students told Òrùnmìlà to choose patience.

When he asked why, they simply replied that Ifá said that the eldest who had patience would have achieved everything.

Òrúnmìlà thanked each of those present and chose patience. Igun then returned to heaven with the remaining gifts. The two wives protested and began to argue with Órùnmìlà. The young woman said that all the good things in life would elude them because Órùnmìlà had made a wrong choice.

The older woman said that Órùnmìlà should have chosen children because nothing was greater than children. The two wives started fighting, both upholding their choice, soon a fight ensued and they started hitting each other. They fought until they were tired, when the wives complained to Órùnmìlà he would simply tell them that whoever had patience would have obtained everything.

While in heaven and yet wealth had grown tired of living in heaven without patience, he came to his head three months later, and wealth went to Olódùmarè to seek permission to go and live patiently in Órùnmìlà's house. Olódúmarè granted his request with this Órùnmìlà became rich, he could support or pay for many things and his young wife became happy.

Three months after this the children went to Olódúmarè to ask permission to keep wealth or patience Olódúmarè granted their request, the two wives became pregnant, the older wife became very happy nine months later the two wives gave birth to healthy children.

Three months later longevity went with Olódúmarè and he sought permission to go live with patience, wealth and children in the land of solitude. Olódúmarè granted his request. Órùnmìlà who chose patience then obtained wealth children longevity as bonuses.

Òrúnmìlà and the guardians of his house became happy, rich and happy, they were singing and dancing and giving praises to Olódúmarè all the Ire of life.

Òpópó t'ìrópó;
Òpòpò t'ìròpò;
Ò fi sééré kan dùùrù;
Ò fi dùùrù kan sééré;
Díá fún Òrúnmìlà;
Yóó se ooree kan ti kò níí mo ìdìi rè;
Wón ní kó sákáalè, ebo ní síse;
Ó gbé'bo, Ó rúbo;
Yóó se oore fún Igún omo Olòdùmarè;
Ó se fún Igún omo Olòdùmarè;
Ó san fún Igún;
Àrùn ti n se Igún ní inú;
Ó san fún Igún;
Ó se fún Igún omo Olòdùmarè;
Ó san fún Igún;
Àrùn ti n be lésè Òtún Igún;
Ó san fún Igún;
Ó se fún Igún omo Olòdùmarè;
Ó san fún Igún;
Àrùn tí nbe lésè òsì Igún;
Ó san fún Igún;
Ó se fún Igún omo Olòdùmarè;

76

Ó san fún Igún;
Àrùn tí nbe lápá òtún Igún;
Ó san fún Igún;
Ó se fún Igún omo Olòdùmarè;
Ó san fún Igún;
Àrùn tí n be lápá òsì Igún;
Ó san fún Igún;
Ó se fún Igún omo Olòdùmarè;
Ó san fún Igún;
Kò pé, kò jìnnà;
E wá bá ni ní jèbútú Ire gbogbo;
Njé mó gbowó mo gbomo;
Mo gbomo tán;
Emi gba àìkú;
Mo gba sùrúrù.

Translation:
Òpópo t'irópó1
Òpópo t'irópó2
He who uses gourd of şẹ̀ẹ̀rẹ̀3 to hit musical instrument of
dùùrù4
He who uses musical instrument of dùùrù to hit gourd of
şẹ̀ẹ̀rẹ̀
They were ones who launched Ifá for Ọ̀rùnmilá
Who will do a great favor that he would not be aware of
They advised him to offer sacrifice
he fulfilled
He would do a favor to the vulture the son of Olódúmarè
He did a favor to cultivate the son of Olódúmarè
He was a relief to the vulture
The ailment in the vulture's stomach
It was a relief to the vulture

77

He did a favor to the vulture the son of Olódúmarè
It was a relief to the vulture
The ailment in the correct leg of vulture
It was a relief to the vulture
He did a favor to cultivate the son of Olódúmarè
It was a relief to the vulture
The ailment in the left leg of the vulture
It was a relief to the vulture
He did a favor to the vulture the son of Olódúmarè
It was a relief to the vulture
The ailment in the right arm of the vulture
It was a relief to the vulture
He did a favor to the vulture the son of Olódúmarè
It was a relief to the vulture
The ailment in the left arm of the vulture
It was a relief to the vulture
He did a favor to the vulture the son of Olódúmarè
It was a relief to the vulture
Before long, not too far
Meet us in the midst of all the IRE in life
Look, I acquire wealth
I buy the children
After acquiring the children
I get long life
And added patience to my gifts
Ifá says that, with patience, wealth, longevity and children
are guaranteed for the client of this Odù.

OGBE OGUNDA VERSE 13

Òní lè n wò;
Ìgbèyìn mi Kàsài tòòrò;
Díá fún Mákanjúolá;

Ti n somo Elérìn Sàjéjé;
Èyí tó fèyìntì mójú ekún sùnráhùn Ire gbogbo;
Wón ní kó sákáalè, ebo ní síse;
Ó gbé'bo, Ó rúbo
Translation:
It is today you are considering
My future will not only be bright and successful
That was the declaration of the oracle Mákanjúolá
Who was the descendant of Elérin Sàjéjé
When crying in regrets of his mistake for having
I will go in life
He was warned to offer sacrifice
he he fulfilled

PROPHESY

Ifá says that the client for whom this Odù is revealed is currently experiencing hardships. Ifá says that his future will be fruitful. No matter what has happened, your problems will go away and give way to success and prosperity, you will have the ire of wealth, children and long life in the future. Before you die, you will become very successful.

Ifá says that the time of success will come. Many people will be wondering how he has managed to achieve success.

Pàtaki

Mákanjúolá, whose name means "do not be in a hurry to acquire honor and wealth", was the son of Elérin, the king of the people of Erin, He had problems. He did not have money. He didn't have a wife. He had no children. He had no home. He had no Ire. They were so sad that one day, he decided to go see Babaláwo near his father's palace. Would this improve his life, judging by his current sorry condition?

The awo told him to put his mind to rest. He told Mákanjúolá that he had a very bright future even though everyone had written that he could not be great in life. The awo told him that Ifá says that he should change that:

Òní lè n wò; Ìgbèyìn mi Kàsài tòòrò

Translation

It is today you are considering

My future will only be bright and successful

He was warned to be hardworking and patient. He complied. Every morning. Mákanjúolá went to his daily work with dedication and determination to succeed.

Much earlier, Mákanjúolá became rich. He was able to marry. The wife gave him many children. Mákanjúolá and his children built a large house of their own and soon after he acquired many horses. He became a very influential person in his community.

One day, when he was riding his horse from his house to Elerin's palace, some people saw him and asked each other about the identity of the influential man riding the horse. When they found out that it was Mákanjúolá of whom everyone had said that he would never be an important person in life, everyone was amazed and surprised. Some of them approached Mákanjúolá to ask him what he had done to become a successful man and when he had acquired his wealth.

Mákanjúolá only told them that the oracle had declared to him "that it was only today you are considering, that the future will only be bright and successful". He was so happy that he began to praise the awo.

Òní lè n wò;
Ìgbèyìn mi Kàsàì tòòrò;
Díá fún Mákanjúolá;
Ti n somo Elérìn Sàjéjé;
Èyí tó fèyìntì mójú ekún sùnráhùn Ire gbogbo;
Wón ní kó sákáalè, ebo ní síse;
Ó gbé'bo, Ó rúbo;
Kò pé kó jìnnà;
Ire gbogbo wá ya dé tùtúru;
Njé Mákanjúolá omo Elérìn Sàjéjé;
Ìwo sì tún padà, o d'olówó;
Ayéè re tutù j'omi lo;
Mákanjúolá omo Elérìn Sàjéjé;
Ìwo sì tún padà, o d'aláya;
Ayéè re tutù j'omi lo;
Mákanjúolá omo Elérìn Sàjéjé;
Ìwo sì tún padà, o d'olówó;
Ayéè re tutù j'omi lo;
Mákanjúolá omo Elérìn Sàjéjé;
Ìwo sì tún padà, o d'onílé;
Ayéè re tutù j'omi lo;

Mákanjúolá omo Elérìn Sàjéjé;
Ìwo sì tún padà, o d'oníre gbogbo;
Ayéè re tutù j'omi lo;
Mákanjúolá o omo Elérìn;
Ìgbà wo lo là tóo lówó?

Translation:
It is today you are considering
My future will not only be bright and successful
That was the declaration of the oracle Mákanjúolá
Who was the descendant of Elérin Sàjéjé
When crying in regrets of his mistake for having
Some will go in life
He was warned to offer sacrifice
he he fulfilled
Time before, not too far
All the Iré of life came together
Now, Makanjuola the descendant of Elérin Sàjéjé
You have changed and become a rich man
Your life is cooler than water
Makanjuola, the descendant of Elérin Sàjéjé
You have changed and you have married
Your life is cooler than water
Makanjuola, the descendant of Elérin Sàjéjé
You have changed and become the father of many children.
Your life is cooler than water
Makanjuola, the descendant of Elérin Sàjéjé
You have changed and you have become a boss
Your life is cooler than water
Makanjuola, the descendant of Elérin Sàjéjé
When did you succeed and become rich?
Ifá says that this client will rise from the grass to grace. On

the other hand, the client must not underestimate anyone. You should never look down on anyone in life. The client must exercise patience and be dedicated in his work. Glory will be his limit.

OGBE OGUNDA VERSE 14

Òpè kú, màrìwò sòsì;
Oko kúkú mó nlólósì obìnrin;
Aya kúkú mó nlólósì okùnrin;
Awo Olúbéte;
Díá fún Olúbéte;
Ó fèyìntì mójú ekún sùnráhùn omo;
Wón ní kó sákáalè, ebo ní síse;
Ó gbé'bo, Ó rúbo

Translation:
The palm tree died; its fronds became useless
The death of the husband is the poverty of the woman (wife)
The death of the wife is the poverty of man
They were the Awos of Olúbéte
They threw Ifá for Olúbéte
When the cry of lamentation of his inability to have a child
You are advised to offer sacrifice
He obeyed.

PROPHESIES

Ifá says that it is advisable for these children of the same parents to offer sacrifice will fester from premature death in this Odù.

83

Ifá says that those who are conspiring to eliminate them are those whose parents of dismayed clients had in one way or another earlier attention. Ifá says that the people who plan the elimination of the client and his brothers are people who find it difficult to show gratitude to Olódúmarè and his affinities for any good that is done to them.

Ifá also says that if the client and his brothers plan to travel outside their place of residence, they must file the plans for the times to come. This is to avoid calamities or premature death.

Ifá further says that this client should never engage in farming or farming activities in any way that would bring you problems in your life on the farm.

This does not mean that you cannot engage in the sales, supply of processed, canned, or finished food items from factories, stores, or warehouses.

Pàtaki

Olúbéte was a prosperous man. He had a wife, but she couldn't have babies with him. As a consequence, he approached the awo mentioned above to consult Ifá.

She was told to him that she would give life to three children before she died. He was also informed that his name would not disappear from the face of the earth when he died. He was asked to offer in sacrifice three pigeons, three guinea fowl, three chickens and money.

He obeyed.

One month he offered the sacrifice, his wife became pregnant and she gave birth to a boy. They called him the boy Emo (mountain rat). Three years later his wife became pregnant again and she gave birth to another child. The boy was called Òyà (grass cutter). Three years later the wife became pregnant and gave birth to yet another child. The child was named Lárìnkà (mouse).

Olúbéte, being a prosperous man gave money to many people in the form of a loan. He also had large farms in different places. Those who were unable to repay the loan had to go to work on the Olúbéte farms until they could repay the loan. Those who owed money included Oká (cobra), Eré (python) and Àgbádú (black snake). They were working on the Olúbéte farms, because they had not been able to collect the loans.

One day, Olúbéte died. A few days after his death, his belongings were divided among his three sons.

Those who owed Olúbéte and could not repay the loans were also assigned among the three children, Emó received Oká, Òyà received Eré while Lárìnkà received Àgbádú.

The three debtors began to work on the farms of the new owners.

The three debtors could not understand why they should serve the father and continue to serve his children after his death. They therefore conspired to kill the three sons.

Oká then, invited Emó to the farm so that he would come to see the progress in it. The same day Eré invited Òyà while Àgbádú invited Lárìnkà to the farm. Their intention was to kill Olúbéte's children as soon as they arrived.

Emo arrived at his farm. He met with Oka. When Emo approached Oka, Emo was struck to death.

Òyà also went to the farm. When Eré saw it, Eré hit Òyà to death.

In the case of Lárìnkà, he went to consult the Ifá of the awo whom his father previously contacted before he was born. He was advised not to go to the farm for some time. He was also told that he should not accept any invitation that he proposed to travel from one place to another for a month. This was because death was lurking somewhere. Therefore, he should stay on his land. However, he was advised to sacrifice a stick (staff), three roosters and money. He had to take them and place them on the way to the farm. He has done as advised.

When Àgbádú waited a few hours and did not see Lárìnkà arrive at the farm, Àgbádú decided to go and find Lárìnkà in his house to kill him. When he realized the place where Lárìnkà had placed the sacrifice, Èsù Òdàra convinced Àgbádú to wait for Lárìnkà there. Èsù Òdàra convinced Àgbádú that Lárìnkà had placed the sacrifice in that place and that Lárìnkà would return to remove the sacrifice in the afternoon. Àgbádú agreed to wait. Meanwhile, Èsù Òdàra went and alerted all the people passing by that there was a dangerous snake lurking on the road to the farm and that the snake could kill them if they did not kill it first.

The passersby approached and saw Àgbádú and used what he had asked for for the sacrifice and used it as material to beat him to death. Oká and Eré also arrived and were also beaten to death.

After Àgbádú's death, Èsù Òdàra went to Lárìnkà's house to warn him and to take him to see the traitors.

Èsù Òdàra told him how his two older brothers had been killed by Oká and Eré. Lárìnkà was so happy that he was able to defeat his enemies. He began to sing, dance and call his Awo:

Òpè kú, màrìwò sòsì;
Oko kúkú mó nlólósì obìnrin;
Aya kúkú mó nlólósì okùnrin;
Awo Olúbéte;
Díá fún Olúbéte;
Ó fèyìntì mójú ekún sùnráhùn omo;
Wón ní kó sákáalè, ebo ní síse;
Ó gbé'bo, Ó rúbo;
Ìgbàti yóó bìí;
Ó bí Emó;
Ìgbàti yóó bìí;
Ó bí Òyà;
Ìgbàti yóó bìí;
Ó bí Lárìnká;

Omo adé'lùú tòyo;

Omo aréyín j'ogún aso;

Olúbéte ló yá oká lérú;

Ó yá Erè ní Iwòfà;

Ó yá Àgbà-dúdú-nìhinìho;

Olúbéte ló wá folójó sàìsí;

Nígbàtí ó kú tán;

Wón mú Oká;

Wón j'ogún rè fún Emó;

Wón j'ogún rè fún Òyà;

Wón wá j'ogún Àgbà-dúdú-nìhonìho;

Fún Lárìnká adélùú tòyo;

Omo aréyín jogún aso;

Oká ló wá pa Emó;

Erè ló pa Òyà je;

Lárìnká ló wá nbe nílè ti nsebo ó;

Njé Oká p'Emó;

Sèké sòdàlè;

Bá mi pá o;

Sèké sòdàlè;

Erè p'Òyà jeo;

Sèké sòdàlè;

Bá mi pá o;

Sèké sòdàlè;

Ó wá kú Lárìnká asé lùú tòyo o;

Sèké sòdàlè; Bá mi pa o; S

èké sòdàlè

Translation:

The palm tree died; its fronds became useless

The death of the husband is the poverty of the woman (wife)

The death of the wife is the poverty of man

They were the Awos of Olúbéte

They threw Ifá for Olúbéte
When the cry of lamentation of his inability to have a child
You are advised to offer sacrifice
He obeyed.
When he gave birth
He gave life to Emó (mountain rat)
When he gave birth
He gave life to Òyà (grass cutter)
When he gave birth
He gave life to Lárìnkà (mouse)
He who came to town and refused to return (to the farm)
He who has a set of teeth as a legacy of beauty.
Olúbéte borrowed Oká (charge) some money to serve him as a slave.
He borrowed from Eré (python) some money to serve him as a vassal
He also borrowed from Àgbádú (black snake) some amount
Olúbéte died later
After his death
They took Oka
And they gave Emo (as a slave)
They took Eré
And they delivered it to Òyà
To Lárìnkà
Oká then he killed Emó
I was a murderer and consumed Òyà
Only Lárìnkà was advised to offer sacrifice
Now, Oka killed Emo
Please help me kill my traitors
Please help
I was a murderer and consumed Òyà
Please help me kill my traitors
Please help

Only Lárìnkà remained
Please help me kill my traitors
Please help
Ifá says that the client for whom this Odú is revealed will
defeat his enemies.

OGBE OGUNDA VERSE 15

A lémo l'ójú àlá ni Ifá njé;
Ó f'èsín, f'òkò lé'mo jò s'ódò Oya;
Ibi wón gbé n ye pápá Ajé de Ògún;
Wón yè'nà aya de Ìja;
Wón yè'nà omo de Òsóòsì;
Wón wá yènà òrun fún baba mi Àgìríílógbón

Translation:
Whoever pursues in the dream of him is what Ifá is known
to be
He uses javelin and spear to chase or hunt one in the Oya
River.
Where they were clearing the field of wealth for Ògún
They cleared the path of a wife for Ìja
They cleared the path of a child for Òsóósì
They however cleared the way to heaven (death) for
Órùnmìlà

PROPHESY

Ifá says that the one who seeks the ire of victory over the
adversary for the client for whom Ogbè-Ìyònú is revealed.
Ifá says that no matter what the client does, he will be subject
without conception and misunderstood for this reason while

people are planning good for others, they will be planning evil for you.

Ifá says that four people were involved in this stanza. While the plans are to assist three other people to be successful, there was a plan to eliminate this client due to lack of conception. Ifá says that the client for whom this odu is revealed, needs to offer sacrifice to cope with death and live long.

Pàtaki

Many people who were close to Órùnmìlà were giving other false information about his activities. They claimed that he was using his Ifá to cause problems for the people, to wreak havoc on others in this wisdom, the people decided to pay him with their own currency.

At the same time, the general opinion was that Ògún, Ìja and Òsóósì were very good for society and that Órùnmìlà was planning evil for the people. They decided to honor Ògún with wealth, Ìja with a wife and Òsóósì with a son. On the other hand, they planned to dispatch Órùnmìlà to heaven.

When Órùnmìlà heard this, he went to meet his students, the students assured him that no one could send him to heaven. He was advised to offer sacrifice with a rooster and a gong. He obeyed. The meaty comb of the rooster was cut and burned with native chalk, camwood, Ape leaves and Igbo leaves. Nine incisions were made on the crown of his head and this powder was rubbed off. His followers did the

91

same. (For a woman seven incisions would be made with a razor blade). The gong was struck every morning.

After doing this, no one was able to harm him, nor his followers. This was how Òrúnmìlà was able to defeat his opponents:

A lémo l'ójú àlá ni Ifá njé;
Ó f'èsín, f'òkò lé'mo jò s'ódò Oya;
Ibi wón gbé n ye pápá Ajé de Ògún;
Wón yè'nà aya de Ìja;
Wón yè'nà omo de Òsóòsì;
Wón wá yènà òrun fún baba mi Àgìríílógbón;
Òrúnmìlà ní tó bá se bí ìse tòhun bá ni;
Éfun kìkí ta kankan kú;
Dùgbè;
Ni ng ó maa rò m'ókùn ayé lo o;
Dùgbè;
Òsùn kìí ta wàràwàrà kó gbòde òrun lo;
Dùgbè;
Ni ng ó maa rò mókùn ayé lo o;
Dùgbè;
Ogbè kìí sí lo lórí àkùko;
Dùgbè;
Ni ng ó maa rò mókùn ayé lo o;
Dùgbè;
Àpè ló ní kí ndá temí pé láyé;
Dùgbè;
Ni ng ó maa rò mókùn ayé lo o;
Dùgbè;
Èlà ló ní kí ndá temí là láyé;
Dùgbè;
Ni ng ó maa rò mókùn ayé lo o;

Dùgbè;
Ìgbó ló ní kí ng dá temí gbé láyé;
Dùgbè;
Ni ng ó maa rò mókùn ayé lo o;
Dùgbè;
Agogo kó máa ró kee;
Èlà má jèé kí won ó fóhùn-un temí kù láílái;
Agogo kó máa ró ke

Translation:
Whoever pursues in the dream of him is what Ifá is known to be
He uses javelin and spear to chase or hunt one in the Oya river.
Where they were clearing the field of wealth for Ògún
They cleared the path of a wife for Ìja
They cleared the path of a child for Òsóòsì
They however cleared the way to heaven (death) for Órùnmìlà
Orunmila said that this was his practice
The native chalk or chalk is never in a hurry to die firmly
I will continue to hang on the rope of life firmly
Camwood is never in a hurry to go to heaven firmly
I will continue to hang on the rope of life firmly
The fleshy crest will never disappear from a rooster's head firmly
I will continue to hang on the rope of life firmly
Ape has sanctioned my long stay on earth firmly
I will continue to hang on the rope of life firmly
She is authorized my experience in life firmly
I will continue to hang on the rope of life firmly
Igbo had authorized my life at my age in life firmly
I will continue to hang on the rope of life firmly

Let the metal-gong seem loud
She may not have allowed them to miss my voice forever.
Let her metal-gong seem to ring loud
Ifá says that he will not allow the client for whom this odu
is revealed to die young.

OGBE OGUNDA VERSE 16

Èeèùú níí ṣ'ẹnu tutuuti s'Ọlọrun;
Bí èyí tí yóó p'ogun;
Bẹẹ no ò léè p'ogun;
Díá fún tiẹ;
Tiẹ n t'ọrun bọ wálé ayé;
Wón ní kí wọn sákáalẹ, ẹbọ ní ṣíṣe;

Translation
Eesuu' is that place for the high sky
Like a cry to invite war
Considered that he cannot be called for war
That he was the only one who threw Ifá for Tiẹ
When he came from heaven to the world
He was asked to offer sacrifice

PROPHESY

Ifá says that the person who comes out of this Odù must
take serious hygiene. The client, if she is a woman, must
always clean the house regularly and sweep the entire house
at least twice a day. She should take a bath, wash her mouth
and take care of personal hygiene at least twice in a day.

Ifá says that when she delivers a baby, her cleaning should be double, this is because her children are allergic to dirt and dust. Sometimes they begin to drag from the environment that is not clean, the child can inhale the dust that can cause the death of the child.

If the woman has a repeated problem of infant mortality, that is not caused by some witch, warlock or evil thing, that was a result of her lack of personal and environmental hygiene.

Pàtaki

Tiẹ was a spirit that lived within dust and dirt. She loved taking human children to heaven. When Tiẹ came into the world, human beings were warned and asked to ensure that the environment was taken care of while personal hygiene was also given a high priority. Many people complied, but those who did not comply would find that their children would die a mysterious death. When asked where their children would be, they replied that the children had continued back to heaven.

Èeèùú níí ṣ'ẹnu tutuuti s'Ọlọrun;
Bí èyí tí yóó p'ogun;
Bẹẹ no ò léè p'ogun;
Díá fún tiẹ;
Tiẹ n t'ọrun bọ wálé ayé;
Wón ní kí wọn sákáalẹ, ẹbọ ní ṣíṣe;
Njẹ ọmọ dà?;
Ọmọ ti bá tiẹ lọ o

Translation

Eesuu' is that place for the high sky

Like a cry to invite war

Considered that he cannot be called for war

That he was the only one who threw Ifá for Tiẹ

When he came from heaven to the world

He was asked to offer sacrifice

Now where is the boy?

The boy returned (to heaven) with Tiẹ

Ifá says that it is in the best interest of the client to take hygiene very seriously.

3- OGBÈ OSÁ; OGBÈ SÁ; OGBÈ SÒÓTOÓ; OGBÈ SOTITO; OGBÈ RI IKU SA

```
+
O I
I I
I I
I I
```

I PRAY:

Ogbèsá Yèyé matero aféfe sá lú Ayé aféfe sá lú Olórun A dífá fún ewé Bana awa jé ní Àgbò, awa jé ni Òrúnmìlà aféfe lona Şàngó A dífá fún ewé Bana.

Ìyere:

Àgbò nsá Àgbò ni jà, Àgbò lo dè igi

IFÁ OF

• Inconsideration
• Trap
• Treason

PROVERBS:

- Gets swagger
- He who betrays his son deserves the same form as the ram
- He who wishes the death of another is because he is dead
- The bad thing you did once, don't do it again
- The light of the moon clears, like the eyes of Olófin, they give clarity to all
- Tree that is born crooked, its trunk never straightens
- Two friends do not admit a third
- Scares, but does not kill
- Make a fist to hit us in the chest
- When a parent dies, there is desolation in the home
- You can be more cunning than another, but not more cunning than others
- If you ate the sauce, you will eat the fish
- All animals are not tied by the necks
- Where there are no elders, there is no government, therefore, when there are no elders, things do not go well

BORN:

- Renal Anuria (Kidney that does not work).
- The house of Ikú and the foundation of Yèwa
- Here the Moon (Oṣupa) was created
- Here the head of Asonyin (Òsányin) was born
- Here was born the casserole or jar of Asonyin
- That whoever has Odùdúwà, should never eat Àgbò
- That in this Odù, the three Eegún Kings are consecrated: Eegún Oba Erun, Eegún Oba Oyigbo and Eegún Oba

Kukunduku

- In this Odù the Atemoleta was consecrated
- That the crown of Òlódùmarè is being prepared
- Here the power to awaken Òrúnmìlà was taken from Ògbè Òsá and it was Ògbè Di

BRAND:

- Mark Betrayal of Friends
- There are traps
- Losses always
- Betrayals

SIGNALIZE

- That here the person is not considered.
- That this Odu the person can become visually ill until they become blind.
- Problem of inflammation in the testicles in men and pelvic inflammation in women.
- Disease of the nerves.

IFÁ SAYS:

- The Throne of Ikú, where you have to kneel to feed Eegún.
- From people who are not friends and used to be.
- From diseases of the heart, instep and neck.
- That he has a very pretty and attractive daughter or woman that everyone looks at.
- Complete works must be done to avoid losses.
- Whenever this sign comes out, Adié is given to Ọya and

Ẹbọ

- You have to receive Kuanado to erase this Ifá
- You have to prepare your stomach for when Ogu eats for this Ifá
- From diseases of the testicles
- To take care of your sight because you can go blind
- Of bad things that have been done and that can be discovered at any time.
- Of problems with the justice
- To have a house or establishment and that it will do well in business
- Of an upset that the person has
- Of gossip, of envy that they can hurt him to see him passing jobs
- That his father is sick (if he is alive) and of spiritual care (if he is dead).
- From falls and leg ailments
- From diseases of the nerves.

PROHIBITIONS

- You don't eat coconut
- The day Awo sees this Ifá, he does not walk with anyone.
- If you make Ẹbọ with Àgbò, the person in question does not eat it.
- Don't trust anyone.

RECOMMENDATIONS

- Receive ifá, or Ọwọ́ fa kán.

- Receive Òṣósii quickly
- During 7 days do not visit sick, there may be a change of heads
- Oborí with Eja tútù (Snapper) and Beer
- Put your money on Ṣàngó, so that he knows what you have
- Set up a small altar for spiritual care, with an Ebony Crucifix.
- The Works or whatever else you are going to do, make them complete so that there are no losses.
- Give food to Eegún
- Put silver handles on Òrúnmìlà inside and also on the Ikofá, if it is Awo, two on each hand of Ifá.
- Make Ẹbọ to avoid a misfortune or have losses in the house
- Give a Ram to Ṣàngó and Àkúko to Yémọjá, so that he can overcome his difficulties.
- Have everyone do Ẹbọ in the family.
- Do not run and do not get into matters that do not concern you
- Give a mass to your father if he is dead
- Don't answer for anyone, so you don't have to pay for others
- Give thanks to Òṣùn and Ṣàngó, who have saved you from many situations
- Beware of bad winds
- Take care of your eyes and testicles
- Hold on to Òrúnmìlà.

EWÉ ODÙ ÒGBÉ ÒSÁ

Ewé Bana (Jabóncillo)	Ceiba Bejuco Jimaguas

PÀTAKI LISTING

1. Here they did not consider Awo Ògbè Sa
2. Ewé Bana the Soap "Jaboncillo"
3. The Trap of the Tiger to the Deer
4. The house of Ikú is born
5. The three Kings
6. The shadow of Eegún Burukú
7. Make all things complete
8. The betrayal of the Ram to the Monkey

WORKS WITH ÒGBÉ ÒSÁ

<u>Work to save the person</u>

A set of tools from Ọya, an Àkúko, Ẹiyelé méjì, indigo, Àsọ ara, Asọ of 9 colors, atitan ilé, eku, eja, epo, Èbìtì, Àgbado, ọpọ̀lọ̀pọ̀ owó.

He is asked if with those things otán (it is enough), otherwise, what he says is added, the

tools are given the way they take.

Òsẹ́ Òtùrà, Ògbè Sa, and Òtùrà Se are painted on a white plate, tools are placed on top, orí and efún, afterwards a little water is added with indigo and Olórun is asked.

Afterwards, the interested party is made Sarayeye with the

102

Àkúko and it is given to the earth, it is buried there and on top, the Ẹbọ and the plate are put on it, this is done behind the interested party's back.

Ẹbọ for the person who is sick in the house

Àkúko, adié méjì, 10 pesos in five-cent coins, 101 marble pebbles, Àṣo ara, measurement of the person's body, the lerí (head), surgical instruments, Aṣó of colors and other ingredients, ọ̀ pọ̀ lọ̀ pọ̀ owó.

Iṣé from Òsányin

A piece of "palo cocuyo" (Firefly stick), changes voice, root of oyu oro, dew of the night, ataare méta, ou, Dúdú and funfun, a 5-cent coin with holes, Iyefá, Àṣọ of the color that takes, is wrapped and lined in the four-colored thread, Òrúnmìlà is asked what he eats and what days they are, if he drinks otín, dry wine, oyu oro (Rain water) or dew of the night.

Artwork for when you see this Odù intorí ikú

The Òpèlè is removed, an Aye de igbin is taken and it is put eku, eja, epo, Iyefá of the Odù and all this is put on Elégbà.

Give Ewúre to Òrúnmìlà and Ọbàtàlá

Note: Intorí ikú (after three days you can die)

Ẹbọ: Àkúko méta, Ekuekueye okàn, Iṣu, Asia, opolopo owó.

103

Ẹbọ: Àkúko fifẹṣu, Ẹiyelé méjì funfun, 10 handles, orí, efun, Ọfà okàn, Iṣu, Àṣo timbè lara, the other ingredients, owó la méjo.

Ẹbọ: Àkúko, Adié, ṣaguro, ide, ou dúdú, the other ingredients, oboyo owó.

Ẹbọ: Àkúko, adíe, Ẹiyelé, ìleké, orí, aponte potika, the other ingredients, owó la meyo.

Ẹbọ: Àkúko fifẹṣu, Ẹiyelé méjì funfun, necklaces beads of Òṣùn, eight necklaces' beads of Ọbàtàlá, Ọfà, Iṣu, karakoa, Àṣo timbè lara, apontepotika, the other ingredients, owó la meyo. Ẹbọ: Àkúko, adié méjì, Ẹtù méjì, Ẹiyelé marùn, ido mésàn, apontepotika (cajón), the other ingredients, owó la mésàn.

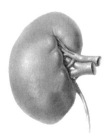 

Born: Renal Anuria (Kidney that does not work).

In Ogbe Osá the Moon (Oṣupà) was created

<u>To Solve Problems with Other People</u>

Make Apayerú with the names and surnames of the araye written on the paper that is smeared with eri, which is placed in the Apayerú package with seven cockroaches from caves and thrown in the bush. When the cockroaches begin to walk and eat the Apayerú with the paper with the names of the araye, restlessness will take over these people.

Elégbà of Ogbè Sá

The Elégbà of Ogbè Sá is mounted on an òtá that has the face of a caravel, it is cemented in a clay ikokó and a male weight is embedded in it. This Elégbà wears a toy Monkey. When assembling him, monkey poles and bones are thrown on him and he is covered with a lot of ewe Eran (hen's feet) and fine grass and 7 Pacific sea flowers.

Èṣù Ṣiki

It is made of dough. In addition to the fundamental elements, it has graveyard soil, two Inkines, lerí from Owunko, Ayá, Agbibo (Cao), and a lot of Quicksilver. It is lined with Elégbà and Òrúnmìlà beads.

Èṣù Katero

This Elégbà is made of dough. In addition to the fundamental ingredients, it contains: Ilèakan, three dark cents, 3 grains of agbadó mora, boil garro, picapica, pendejera, ekú, eja, epó, otín, erú, kolá, osun, 13 ataré. The blade is loose in the ikokò.

Òsányin of Ogbè Sá

Take a piece of palo cocuyo, change voice, eyero root, tie,

mate, black and white thread, 5 cents from Hole, a little Iyefá from this Odù, cloth of the color you pick, lined with 54-color thread, Òrúnmìlà is asked what he eats and what days it is, and what he drinks, if oti, parrot, oyouro, and night dew.

Other Işé

It carries in a monkey leather bag, Iyefá of the sign, sea sand, lerí gunugun, lerí de Gavilán, lerí de Cao, obí, eru, kola, olelé, and an iddé of Òrúnmìlà. Eat together with Òrúnmìlà.

Work of Ogbè Sá:

The Ewe Bana is the little soap. First you have to give two birds to Òsányin giving him accounts of the work to be done, then the leaves of the ewé are placed on top of Òsányin and he is given coconut. Then these leaves are collected and an omiero is made with them. You are asked to lerí the interested party with eiyelé méjì funfun and then the promotion begins to be applied to the damaged parts. They also cure hemorrhoids, also in promotion.

Work to save the person

A set of Oya tools, an Àkúko, Eiyelé méjì, indigo, aşo arae, aşo of 9 colors, atitan Ilè, eku, eja, epo, Èbìtì, àgbado, opolopo owó.

He wonders if he ota with those things, otherwise what he picks up, the tools the way they take, is added.

Òşé Tùrà, Ogbè Sá, and Òtùrà Şé are painted on a white

106

plate, the tools, orí and efún are placed on top, then a little water with indigo is added to the plate and Olórun is asked. Afterwards, Sarayeye is made for the interested party with the Àkúko and it is given to the ground, it is buried right there and the ẹbọ and the plate are placed on top of it, this is done behind the interested party's back.

Work to cure sight

Omiero of ewé Atori (Pasiflora), Mora grass, Ewé Tètè Nifá, ewé karoldo (Canutillo), sea and river water, Ogbè Sá is prayed and Iyé is prayed, obí omí tútù is given to Òsányin and Şàngó asking him if nothing is missing, Şàngó how many days does he have to be at his feet and how many days does the person have to wash his eyes.

ẸBỌ:

A box with 9 manillas, Àkúko, whole obí, ewé yarako, a stake, abo hair, aşọ arae, Èbìtì, atitan Ilè, aşọ timbè lara, atitan bata, eku, epo, eja, àgbado, opolopo owó.

ẸBỌ for the person who is sick in the house

Àkúko, adié méjì, 10 pesos in media, 101 marble stones, aşọ arae, body measurement, from the lerí, surgical instruments, colored aşọ, other ingredients, opolopo owó.

ẸBỌ: Àkúko méta, Ekuekueye okàn, Işu, Asia, opolopo owó

ẸBỌ:

Àkúko fifeṣu, Ẹiyelé méjì funfun, 10 handles, orí, efún, ọfà okàn, Iṣu, aṣọ timbè lara, others ingredients, owó la meyo.

ẸBỌ:

Àkúko, Adié, ṣaguero, ide, ou dundun, others ingredients, oboyo owó.

ẸBỌ:

Àkúko, Ekuekueye (not killed, Yémọjá is taken to the sea), a blue and white Asia (given to the person), Iṣé méjì, Ẹiyelé méjì, a bag of beans Caritas, àgbado, others ingredients, opolopo owó.

ẸBỌ:

Àkúko, adié, ẹyin adié, aṣọ funfun, pupa, dudu, ogue de nitiwado, others ingredients, opolopo owó.

ẸBỌ:

Àkúko, adié méjì, ẹtu méjì, Ẹiyelé márun, ido mésàn, apontepotika (drawer), others ingredients owó la mésàn.

ẸBỌ:

Àkúko, adíe, Ẹiyelé, ìleké, orí, apontepotika, others ingredients, owó la méjo.

ẸBỌ:

Àkúko fifeṣu, Ẹiyelé méjì funfun, five beads of Òṣùn, eight beads of Òbàtála, ọfà, Iṣu, karakoa, aṣọ timbè lara, apontepotika, others ingredients, owó la meyo.

ẸBỌ:

Àkúko, abo, Abeboadie, ẹyin adié, aṣọ funfun, dudu y pupa, others ingredients, owó mésàn (the owó is not spent, it is placed on top of Ṣàngó to know what is done with it).

Iṣé de Òsányin

A little piece of palo cocuyo, change voice, root of oyu oro, dew of the night, atare méta, ou, dudu and funfun, a 5-cent coin with holes, Iyefá, asho of the color that it takes, it is wrapped and covered in the thread of four colors, Òrúnmìlà is asked what he eats and what days it is, if he drinks oti, dry wine, oyu oro (Rainwater) or night dew.

Artwork for when you see this Odù intori ikú

The Òpèle is removed, an Aye of igbin is taken and eku, eja, epo, Iyefá of the Odù is put on it and all this is put on Elégbà.

From Ewúre to Òrúnmìlà and Òbàtála

Note: Intori ikú (after three days you can die)

Work: When there is a strong war, an abo is given to

109

Şàngó with an old rooster, the rooster is taken to the foot of Iwí ope (palm)

Òsányin Yuan

This Òsányin is from Ogbè Sá to succeed in life.

Lerí from Ekuekueye, from Ekutele, from Ayandono, the nails of the Àkúko, from Ògún, garbage from the Ilè, scraping of two Ikines of Ifá (one from each hand), root of Ikines, broken ax burned, steel filings, Iyefá scraping del Elégbà, 101 atare, chain, a chamois rod. This one eat Eiyelé, Àkúko, lives hanging from the chain, behind the street door.

OGBÈ SÁ PÀTAKI 1 WHERE THEY DID NOT CONSIDER AWO OGBÈ SÁ.

I PRAY: Ogbè Sá ayanajo òrun oni bawa

Şàngó, o bani bajé omo alara ateni bokun aféfe sá lú ayé aféfe sá lú ó lórun, aye ni late Bábà kolu méjì Ogbè de Olórun láye ewi wa enifá, omo alara Şàngó dede logun ifá tètè eni wa ni láye Òşè Tùrà mo je ni ifá Ogbè Sá Yèyé matero ron lonfe, awa ni aféfe sá lú ayé eri ni yae oşe niré eti wa Òlódùmarè wa male ji ko tun eledifá inlé yeyene, Elégbà, eti ni wa iyo kolun noje Bábà tètè ati ré nifá, Bábà eyi de Ifá orí.

EBO:

etu méjì, akuaro méjì, eja, gbogbo igi, gbogbo ewé, Eiyelé, obí painted in 4 colors, obí with orí and efún, an Àwòran who dresses in strips of all colors and eats with Şàngó, etu, eja, àgbado, epo, oti, land from different places, jar, bait, arrow, opolopo owó

Before making the ẹbọ, a ceremony is performed that is a circumference and Ṣàngó is put to eat with Ògún and it is written, dundun eobon sé lefh efún yori epo and the Odù Éjìogbè, Ogbè Sá and Òṣè Tùrà are put on.

The Ayapá is presented calling Olórun, Ṣàngó and Ògún well, she is given Òṣè Tùrà and the Iyere is sung to her:

Eegún ni mawa Òṣè Tùrà
Eyi ni láye Ayapá Eegún
Malekun Ṣàngó malele
Eegún Malekun.

The two doves are caught and they present themselves well calling all the saints and they are given Éjìogbè singing the Iyere: Eegún Eye Ẹiyelé

Kuarulo Eegún Kuarulo

Take the ẹtu and speak well to Ṣàngó and call Ògún in this way:

Ṣàngó Bábà ó ni láye Eegún
Òwònrìn ó lórun Ṣàngó Bábà eri láyeo
ini lulu gun ara oso bi ri ko ọba ni láye
Kawo Ko bíri Agogo ni láye Kabio, Kabio Sile
The banana is killed and it is said:
Sara yeye Eegún Ṣàngó
Eegún Berun lo rú ne ṣu ni láyeo
Ogbè Sá ni láyeo

Òṣè Tùrà ni láyeo
Bábà Éjìogbè ni láyeo

Pàtaki:

On this road Ogbè Sá was born in the land of Eleni Láye
and his mother was called Ayanao Òrùn, and she was very
upset because on earth they did not want to pay attention to
her, and they did not look at her son Ogbè Sá, the children
of ọmọ Éjìogbè, they presumed of doing and being wise, she
got sad and wondered why they didn't put him on the board,
she blessed him every day and always fed him Ayapá Tiropo,
Amalá and Ilá and they always called Ṣàngó.

Lo ono Éjìogbè were those who saw, ate the ẹtu and bathed
in yellow plums, and the mother named Ayani Láye took her
son ọmọ alara, dressed him in black, took him to where
Òrúnmìlà was and Ogbè Sá saw him and he marked the
previous ẹbọ and did it for him and, finishing the ẹbọ,
different figures appeared and they all spoke of their powers,
at that moment Ṣàngó appeared, wrapped in candle and
singing: Aika Fiku Aye Enifá. Òrúnmìlà who saw this came
out in his company giving Moforibale to Ṣàngó and said:
Agogo ni láye agogo nifá.

Ṣàngó knelt in front of Òrúnmìlà and gave him Moforibale,
he asked for a large jícara with Laguer and put an Edun in it
and began to moyugbar calling Òṣè Tùrà and said:

Òṣè Tùrà ẹbọ ọmọ ni láye

112

Òṣè Tùrà awa tètè le ré ní ifá

Òṣè Tùrà Abe ni lawó Obírin Bokun ọmọ alara Orí Bokun

Orí lòna, Agba la de ni awa tètè losa beye daba kue le

Méjì Erie Eku basu láye.

Òṣè Tùrà appeared, and said: Let's go, he carried Ogbè Sá and took him to the secret of Abo Kulambe Boku Oti Lórun together with Ṣàngó and his Ìyá, Ṣàngó before leaving said to Òrúnmìlà, when I get to consecrate Ogbè Sá , it is necessary to take away the power that Éjìogbè has so that he can share it with Ogbè Sá and Òrúnmìlà told him: Àṣe To Àṣe Bo Àṣe Berin Ni Ifá, Ṣàngó was happy in front of Òrúnmìlà and left the road and arrived at the land of Eleni Láye, and the children of Éjìogbè who saw him were frightened and went to where their father was, Ṣàngó entered singing:

Bábà Éjìogbè tútù láye enifá

Bábà àṣe to awa ni ari bayc orí enifá

He put Ogbè Sá together with Éjìogbè and gave ẹtu méjì to the two heads, Ṣàngó ate akuaró and told him: Éjìogbè has more power than you and Éjìogbè told him: I will never get along with him.

OGBÈ SÁ PÀTAKI 2 EWÉ BANA THE JABONCILLO (SOAP).

I PRAY:

Adífáfún Òrúnmìlà işon şon lade gbogbo aiye inlé ọba Olófin aru je káfírèfún bara petu Lodafún Òsányin.

ẸBỌ:

Ẹiyelé méjìtwo birds that have been hunted, leaves of jaboncillo, gbogbo tenujen, others ingredients y opolopo owó.

Pàtaki:

Òrúnmìlà was touring the world and he arrived at a land where epon aro and ofojude were, where he found himself with swollen testicles and almost blind and Olofin had offered a reward to whoever managed to cure him, but to whoever did not, he offered otokú.

Òrúnmìlà called in this story Ogbè Sá, was under a tired tree and was almost falling asleep after a long walk, when he heard the voice of two birds talking to each other, Òrúnmìlà understood the speech of the birds and one of them he said to the other, so many people who have died to cure the king and do not know that, with the leaves of this tree, the ọba can be cured of his illnesses.

When the Birds had gone, Ogbè Sá took branches from that tree and appeared before the court asking permission to cure the ọba. Olófin who was there told him: Òrúnmìlà you know that if you don't heal him your death is certain.

Ogbè Sá performed the corresponding and precise ceremony and applied the promotion of that omiero to the eyes and testicles of the ọba, after a few hours the improvement was immediately noticed and the next day the ọba was almost well. Olofin seeing that granted all the wealth to Òrúnmìlà and told him: with you there is no one who can.

OGBÈ SÁ PÀTAKI 3 THE TRAP OF THE TIGER TO THE DEER.

Pàtaki

On this road, the Tiger was a staunch enemy of the Deer and at all costs he wanted to eat the Deer.

For his dream, the Tiger devised a trap with the other ferocious animals of the forest, which consisted of playing dead and all the other animals had to spread the word that the Tiger had died, so that the weak animals would go to his funeral and so you can hunt them.

The burial was prepared and they spread the word of the death of the Tiger, the word spread throughout the forest until it reached the Deer, already in the tomb that they had prepared for the Tiger they realized that the Deer had not attended the funeral and They were half disoriented.

They all moved away from the Tiger and made a circle around him so that they could fall on the smaller animals when they appeared.

But it turns out that the Deer had smelled that something was wrong and did not let the other animals go to the funeral, it was only him, and he came at full speed surprising everyone who did not expect him, that way he approached the supposed corpse of the Tiger putting the front left leg on the chest, that leg is the most sensitive, and thus it detected the vibrations of the Tiger's heart, it quickly left like a waterspout giving the voice to the other animals.

When the beasts saw this, they forgot about the other animals and fell on top of the Tiger, they could not reach the Deer, and thus they were left without prey, they were left without a feast, nor did the Tiger carry out its purposes.

OGBÈ SÁ PÀTAKI 4 THE HOUSE OF IKÚ WAS BORN.

I PRAY:

Ogbè Sá ọba bori bokun larose Ìyá toku ọba oni Òṣé ọba niré agba Ifá ore boko lore oni Ogbè Sá orí yeyekun ọba awó yere ri eygun to ni lo oni lòna agba odiba Òlódùmarè lerí àgbo ni afo lowa Ifá la niré Òrúnmìlà ni Olórun owa tokun mo tokun Odùdúwà ọba du ore awó arara Ifá ni Yèwa ayèyé ma pa lowa lerí ikú hépa ọba ní ré wa.

ẸBỌ:

Etu méta, Osiadié méta, Ẹiyelé méta, aworin méta, árbol Ìyá tatu okàn, aṣọ Ọṣẹ boilete, eko, eku, eja, àgbado, opolopo owó.

Ewé: purple basil, Yanten, leaves of Álamo, leaves of Guacalote.

Pàtaki:

In the land of Ọba Bori Bokun, the stench of Eegún could not be tolerated and the different epidemics were spreading throughout the world and most of the people were sick with nerves.

Awo Ifá Ọba Guirere, lived with her iyare, who was called Ọba Oni Òṣà who was raising a girl, who was called orí yeye and Awo Ifá Ọba Guirere lived in love with orí yeye, since she was a child.

Awo's iyare in a certain way was always calling Awo Ifá Ọba Guirere's attention and she replied that he loved her like a sister, until one day, her iyare Ọba oni Òṣé went to visit Odùdúwà, he got upset and He told her, why you have come alone, you know the danger that you have above, and what I am going to return to you, so that you serve the world and make a great foundation of Orìṣa, Odùdúwà began to sing and pray:

Ọbani Òṣé Eegún,

117

Eegún ọba ọbani Òṣé agba
Lerí hépa ko kun ma wa
Ko kun lerí ó Boni
Orí yeye hépa,
hépa lerí hépa
ma wa ko kun.
Ọba Oni Òṣé, was transformed and was singing along the way:
Eegún Oku Olórun Eegún
Agba Oun Moriyeye
Eegún Agba Tokun.

When he arrived in his land, which is the land of ọba Bori Bokun, he found his son with the fault he was committing, the mistake, but Oriyeye blamed himself, a hole was opened in the ground and the two fell inside and told him To Awo Ifá ọba Guirere, you will always have to come to pray and ask this foundation, which is going to be promoted from Lerí Òṣà, but you have to give an account to Olófin, she got scared and started crying, but she (the Eegún of them) started to sing:

Tokun, Tokun Agba Osaire Lerí Òṣà

Osire Aboide Agba Okùn Yèwa.

And snails began to come out of the earth and do things, but he did not want Olofin to know anything about what was happening and Olofin was seeing him, Odùdúwà had already reached where Olofin was and talking to him and Olofin was happy because he was going to meet a great secret within the religion.

Olofin seeing that Awo Ifá ọba Guirere had not come to where he was to tell him about the great secret that his Iyare gave him, he cursed him and began to have a hard time and he was going to ask his Iyare and he did not understand, until he He was so desperate and had to get to where Olofin was and he told him: You will be the one who will do Ilè Eegún, so that everyone knows where the great foundation of the great Òrìṣà is and he began to sing and pray.

Awo Kaleleo ọba Awo Kaleleo ọba Awo Mayere Ikú Eegún Oboniré Ikú Awo Baswkeo awó.

And at the time this became àgbo ọbariafo became goat and came the great happiness for the foundation of Yèwa.

OGBÈ SÁ PÀTAKI 5 THE THREE KINGS.

I PRAY:

ọba Eegún méta, awa je ifá ọmọfá a je wé inlé ogere adé mi ọba eru Eegún ọba Oyigbo, Eegún ọba ku kun du ku ewa oni Eegún ako lome o yi sá aféfe Eegún, Adífáfún òrun, Eegún lodafún Òrúnmìlà, káfírèfún Oluo popo.

EBỌ:

· Adié (negra, blanca y jabada), 3 malaguidí ọkọnrin, Oro, Plata, Cobre, Oka, Akará, Iṣú okàn, Ikokó, Kalalú, Ajiako y

119

opolopo owó.

Note:

In this Odù, 3 Adié are given to Olófin, one each day, first the white, 2nd the black, and 3rd the Jabada. The ẹbọ of Ogbè Sá always carries the three métales, Ogbè Sá must always have a pot from Ajiako to Eegún, to obtain something important, 3 malaguidí are consecrated, one black, one white and one mestizo.

Pàtaki

In the Ayebi Inlé land lived an Awó called Adebi, who always had problems in his town, because it was a land of envy and war, where he was tired of advising them to live in peace.

One day, as they did not pay attention to him, a very big war broke out and there was a great mortality in the town, where Adebi Awó Ogbè Sá left the town and took refuge in the mountain, after walking a lot he reached the foot of a hill, he saw on that hill there was a hole that was the entrance to a cave, he entered and saw that it looked like a house and had three corridors that each led to a room. The first had a gold door, the second silver and the third copper and from each room smells of food came and Adebi Awó Ogbè Sá decided to go to the room that had the copper door because of the rich aroma that came from there. . What Adebi Awó Ogbè Sá did not know was that everything that happened came to the minds of the three inhabitants instantly. When Adebi

Awó Ogbè Sá was heading for that door, all three opened and he was amazed when he saw three men coming out of them wearing clothes and jewelry, according to the metal of that room, those men each had an Adé that identified them as Kings and each one wanted Adebi Awó Ogbè Sá to be their slave.

Then they began to influence the mind of Adebi Awó Ogbè Sá, it was so great that he became disturbed, finally Adebi Awó Ogbè Sá decided on the copper ọba. But those other two ọba Eegún were not satisfied and decided to finish off Adebi Awó Ogbè Sá, but then he became osode and his Ifá was seen, he made the ẹbọ and when he placed it at the foot of a Moruro tree, Asójaanú presented it to him, who He told him: Now when berry fights between those three ọba Eegún you call me and I will help you. When the fight was bigger Adebi Awó Ogbè Sá called Asójaanú, who arrived where the three ọba Eegún were and called them, he asked them, what was happening? And they replied that they wanted to have Adebi Awó Ogbè Sá as a slave so that he could serve as an interpreter on earth, then Asójaanú told them: You three will be able to protect him, but only I and Ṣàngó rule over him, therefore, you have to respect that, and then the three ọba Eegún stayed guarding Adebi Awó Ogbè Sá and his crown took turns with him, thanks to Asójaanú.

OGBÈ SÁ PÀTAKI 6 THE SHADOW OF AN EEGUN BURUKU.

I Pray:

Ogbè Sá Ogbè Yono, oti ikú, ati la bi ja, Ogbè sá pa ra basa pa sá, pa sá okikan ki dubulo ikú, buro ọmọ şuban boro Ọmọ didé

ẸBỌ:

Àkúko Ìkóodíde, adié méjì, Ẹiyelé méjì, ewé okikan, ewé Oya-ko, ewé Tètè Nifá, Igba Omí Okun eku, eja, àgbado, obí, opolopo owó.

Pàtaki

Ogbè Sá was a man who liked to drink Aguardiente very much, and when he drank, he beat himself up in public places, made paper blows and mistreated loved ones. All this was the product of a very bad Eegún that covered him with his shadow when he drank.

Ogbè Sá, seeing that he could not continue in that situation, decided to go to Òrúnmìlà's house, who made him osode, seeing him Ogbè Yono, where Òrúnmìlà told him: What ẹbọ had to do, to go to the foot of a Jobo bush, with a igba of omí and obí and two Ẹiyelé were given. After Ogbè Sá did everything that Òrúnmìlà marked him, he was able to remove the shadow of that Eegún, and had to give up the vice of drinking. Note: When Awó Ogbè Sá left Ogbè Yono,

122

this work or ceremony should be done. Awó Ogbè Sá must wear Deer Leather Sandals.

OGBÈ SÁ PÀTAKI 7 MAKE ALL THINGS COMPLETE

Pàtaki

There was a hunter who had not hunted for several days, and therefore he wondered the reason for this, reflecting, he decided to go to Òrúnmìlà's house, who made him osode and sent him ẹbọ.

The hunter went the next day to Òrúnmìlà's house to make the ẹbọ, but he only had half of what was necessary.

Then the Deer arrived and told Òrúnmìlà that he did not have a moment of rest because of the hunter, Òrúnmìlà made him bear and sent him and sent him the same prayer, and he brought him half.

A few days later the very sad Deer appeared, and told Òrúnmìlà that they had killed his son the hunter, Òrúnmìlà told him to rejoice, because the prayer had been half done and that it had not been enough for him. Later the hunter appeared complaining that among the deer he saw, he hunted the smallest. Òrúnmìlà replied rejoice, because the ẹbọ you did, you did it halfway and settle for what you hunted.

Note: Make things complete.

OGBÈ SÁ PÀTAKI 8 THE BETRAYAL OF THE RAM TO THE MONKEY.

Pàtaki

The Cat and the Dog were together in the house. But the time came when the Dog ate the Cat's food. And this one could not stop at the house, because the Cat had already scratched the Dog to take away his food. The Cat decided to go to the mountain to see the Tiger, to give him an account of what the Dog had done. The Tiger called the Lion to tell him about the Dog. And both beasts agreed to give a big party and a meal. Where they invited all the animals, including the Ram and the Monkey, who were great friends. But neither of them attended because the ram said: That the larger animals were chasing them to eat them, and the Monkey said: That he wanted to because he climbed the trees and ate all the ripe fruits. On the day of the meal the branch of the Lion arrived first and they got the better part. And when the branch of the Tiger arrived, the war began between all the animals, except the Elephant, which, as it came very calmly, arrived last. In these conditions Olofin asked, why were they fighting? and they answered that they were very complaining, and that the fight was due to the great scarcity of food, because the Monkeys ate everything from the Bushes and they did not have enough. Then Olofin sent for the Monkey, and knowing that the Ram was a friend of the Monkey, they promised him that they would not bother him anymore if he managed to bring him, the ram promised to bring him, he made a trap, a chain and a muzzle, a rope and coconuts. But the Monkey had already looked at Òrúnmìlà. And this had ordered him to beg his head three days in a row and not go out on the street, because there was a trap and betrayal. When the Ram arrived at the Monkey's house, his wife did not let him in and told him: That he was not there, that he should leave because the monkey was not in the house and it was not known when he would return. But the Ram at the gate set the trap. And when the Monkey knew that his friend the Ram was there, he went to the door to see him and the Ram told him, I came to see you to bring you these coconuts and when he went to get them, the Monkey fell into the trap, where he tied him up and he gagged him taking him away. Already when he was walking past the hills, the Monkey evoked the high and low regions, imploring Yanza. Then the earth opened up and a volcano came out with a lot of fire, which burned the mooring rope and saved the Monkey. When the ram appeared before Olofin, he told him that he was going to leave the search for the Monkey, but since Olofin already knew the truth, he ordered Ogun to cut off the Ram's head.

4- TRADITIONAL IFÁ OGBE OSA

OGBE OSA VERSE 1

Bí ojù bá n pon Bábálawo;
Kí Babalawo má puró;
Bí ojú bá n pón Onísègùn;
Kí onísègùn má sèra;
K'éni má sèké, sèra;
Nítorí àti sùn Awo;
Díá fún Òrúnmìlà
Níjó eni Àìmo wá n kó ogun ja Baba;
Wón ní kó sákáalè, ebo ní síse;
Ó gbé'bo, Ó rúbo

Translation:
If a Bábálawo is in dire need
Allow the Bábálawo not to lie
If a botanist is in need
Let the botanist not be dishonest
Allow neither a lie nor display dishonesty
These are the declarations of Ifá to Òrúnmìlà

When unknown people (fake, hypocrite) was waging war
They advised him to offer sacrifice
He complied.

PROPHESY

Ifá says that no matter what condition you may be in, you will never

They must fall into traps. You must never cheat or be dishonest. Ifá says

that those who are scamming the person will be found guilty in the end.

Pàtaki

Òrúnmìlà was in an extremely difficult situation, he had two conclusions found. He tried many things that he knew, but none to no avail.

He was always telling people to be firm, honest and sincere. but he was unsuccessful. His honesty did not pay him any good dividend.

On the other hand, all those who were dishonest were very successful. They had all the enviable things in life. They were making all joke of Òrúnmìlà that, despite his honesty, he had a total failure. Therefore, Òrúnmìlà went to the group of Awo mentioned above for the Ifá consultation. The Awo I inform Òrúnmìlà that he must continue displaying transparent honesty in all the thoughts, speeches and deeds of him. They also informed him that he could overcome his problems and, in the future, get to the root of his problems for find out what and who was responsible for his lack of success.

Òrúnmìlà was therefore advised to offer a sacrifice of two hens, two pigeons and money He complied. They then told him to be careful and patient.

A few days after the sacrifice, some of the apparently successful people who were compromised in falsehood came to Òrúnmìlà to advise him so that he would stop being honored since they were really ungrateful. They ordered Òrúnmìlà to consider putting little lies into the business so that he would be successful. Òrúnmìlà did not consider his advice at all and told them that they must remember that we would all be responsible to Olódùmarè at the timem that he or she died. He said that he would continue to be truthful despite his

needs of him. They got upset and left him.

Soon, however, many of them seized and represented Òrúnmìlà defrauding people and obtained various sums of money from them. Many

They were caught stealing. Many others were caught blackmailing. Some they were discovered for demanding to possess a certain privilege or authority that did not belonged. All of them were punished appropriately.

At the same time, the qualities of Òrúnmìlà were recognized and for this reason, he was respected, honored and became the "Oloooto Ayé" - The honored man of the world.

He was very happy and he was praising his Awo like this:
Bí bá n pon Bábálawo;
Kí Bábálawo má puró;
Bí ojú bá n pón Onísègùn;
Kí onísègùn
má sèra;
K'éni má sèké, sèra;
Nítorí àti sùn Awo;
Díá fún Òrúnmìlà;
Níjó eni Àìmo wá
n kó ogun ja Baba;
Wón ní kó sákáalè, ebo ní síse;
Ó gbé'bo, Ó rúbo;
Njé eni Àìmò
Èmi mà wá mò yín o;
Eni Àìmò; Èmi ti mo Mónúmónú;
Tó finú jo Oká; Eni Àìmò
Èmi mà wà mò yín o;
Eni Àìmò;
Èmi ti mo Àgbàdú;
Tó finú jo Erè;
Eni Àìmò
Èmi mà wá mò yín o;
Eni Àìmò;
Emi ti Ìwowo-Erékè;
Tó finú jo Barapetu;
Eni Àìmò

Èmi mà wá mò yín o;
Eni Àìmò
Translation:
If a Bábálawo is in dire need
Do not allow the Bábálawo to lie
If a botanist is in need
Don't let the botanist be dishonest
Do not allow a lie or display dishonesty
Because of the responsibility when he dies
These are the declarations of Ifá to Òrúnmìlà
When unknown persons (hypocrites) were waging war against
he
They advised him to offer sacrifice
He complied.
Now the fakers of yè
You have been exposing everyone
Ye hypocrite
I now know the Python
What pretended in the likeness of the Viper of Gabon
Ye hypocrite
You have been exposing everyone
Ye hypocrite
I recognize the Àgbádú now
What pretended in likeness of the Boa Constrictor
Ye hypocrite
You have been exposing everyone
Ye hypocrite
I can now see through Iwowo-Ereke (Copycat)
Who claimed that he was Òrúnmìlà
Ye hypocrite
You have been exposing everyone
Ye hypocrite

131

Ifá says that his honesty will be rewarded while the liars, hypocrites and imitators will therefore have to be punished.

OGBE OSA VERSE 2

Puró-puró kú;
Ó kú s'ígbó iná;
Sìkà-sìkà kú;
Ó kú s'odàn Òòrùn;
Soto-sòótó kú
Ó kú gbedemuke;
Ó fèyìn ti àmù ìlèkè;
Orunmila Awo Ayé;
Díá fún omo Araye
Nígbàtí wón n se ayé;
Tí ayé kò rójú;
Tí ayé kò jo;
Wón ní kó sákáalè, ebo ní síse
Olóòótó nìkan ní nbe l'éyìn tó n sebo.
  Translation:
  The liar died
But he died in the forest of fire
the bad guy died
But he died in the savannah of the scorching sun
The truthful one died
But he died peacefully
Reclining in a beaded jewelry pot of water
Òrúnmìlà, the Awo of the world,
He was the one who launched Ifá for the inhabitants of this world
When they were living in a world
where there was no peace

where there was no harmony
They were advised to offer sacrifice
Only the truthful (true) complied.
The world was in total chaos. Nothing of work. people were dying of
mysterious ways. Some died pathetic deaths. others in
tragic circumstances. Only a few died peacefully.
Consequently, the
inhabitants of the world chose some representatives among themselves to go to
Òrúnmìlà for the consultation of Ifá.

PROPHESY

Ifá says that you should ALWAYS be honest and truthful in everything you do.

It is the only way you will die well and leave enviable memories for your

offspring.

Pàtaki

Òrúnmìlà told them that they came because there was no peace in the world. He he said it was because of his wickedness and lack of truthfulness. He asked them to go back to their respective houses and change for the better. They must abandon dishonesty and evil and embrace the truth. He said that truthfulness was the only thing he

would bring back peace in the world.

133

All of them all went back to their homes and found it very difficult to be honest and truthful. They soon understood that it was not more convenient to lie, cheat and to be bad than to be truthful and virtuous. Only very few people were able to dwell for the order of Òrúnmìlà. Those were only a few whom the Deity gave his support.

They were only a few who were able to overcome the lows of life.

Puró-puró kú;
Ó kú s'ígbó iná;
Sìkà-sìkà kú;
Ó kú s'odàn Òòrùn;
Soto-sòótó kú Ó kú gbedemuke;
Ó fèyìn ti àmù ìlèkè;
Orunmila Awo Ayé;
Díá fún omo Araye
Nígbàtí wón n se ayé;
Tí ayé kò rójú;
Tí ayé kò jo;
Wón ní kó sákáalè, ebo ní síse Olóòótó nìkan ní nbe l'éyìn tó n sebo.
Njé sotito, sòdodo;
Soore, má sìkà Òtító a bona tóóró;
Òsìkà a bona gbàràrà;
Sotito, Sòdodo;
Sòdodo, Sòtító Eni tó sòtító ní Imolè n gbé.

Translation:
the liar died
But he died in the forest of fire

134

the bad guy died
But he died in the savannah of the scorching sun
The truthful one died
But he died peacefully
Reclining in the beaded jewelry pot of water
Òrúnmìlà, the Awo of the world,
He was the one who launched Ifá for the inhabitants of this world
When they were living in a world
where there was no peace
where there was no harmony
They were advised to offer sacrifice
Only the truthful fulfilled
Pray, be truthful, be virtuous
Do good and don't be bad
Truth, the traveler on the narrow road,
Evil, the traveler in the wide way,
Be truthful, be virtuous
Be virtuous, be truthful
One who is truthful secures the support of the Deity.

Ifá says that only the true and virtuous will receive support from the Deity. Those are the ones They will die peacefully.

OGBE OSA VERSE 3

Bí Irì eni kò pa'ni;
Obà kan kò leè pa'ni;
Díá fún Alundùndùn ilé Olófin;
Nígbàtí nbe
nínú idààmu ayé;
Wón ní kó sákáalè, ebo ní síse;
Ó gbé'bo, Ó rúbo

Translation:
If one's Ori doesn't kill one
no king can be killed
This was the declaration of the Oracle to the drum of
Dùndún in the palace of Olofin
When he was faced with tribulations
They asked him to offer sacrifice
He complied.

PROPHESY
Ifá says that his ORÍ is his support. As long as his ORÍ is
calm, it will be his support,

no one can harm or kill you. The person just needs to be

performing rituals to their ORÍ regularly.

Pàtaki

Dúndùn's drum was Olofin's drum. His preferred name was
"Bí el Orí eni kó pani, Obà kan kò lee pa'ni" (If one's Orí
does not kill one, no King can).

The drum was very popular with this name. One day, some
of Olofin's chiefs they considered this favorite name as an
affront to Olofin. They said that the drum chose that
favorite name as a deliberate effort to ridicule the King.
Therefore, they confronted the King and asked him to take
and give a decisive step to curb the outrage of the drum
urgently.

The drum was summoned to the presence of Olofin. He

was asked why he chose to answer such an arrogant favorite name in the presence of Olofin. He replied that it was not his own making and that this was Ifá's statement to him as long as he went for Ifá consultation. The drum was then asked if whether or not he believed the statement. He replied that he did. This angered the King and the boss of him who decided to teach the drummer a lesson he would not have forgotten early. Drum was asked to go home.

The next day, the drummer was once again summoned to the palace. Olofin gave the

drum his (Olofin) expensive ring to keep for seven days. The ring must

return to the palace on the eighth day. Failure to do this will be punished with

instant death. The drum left the palace.

On arriving home, the drummer called in his two wives and narrated his experience to them.

After this, he sought advice from him on where to keep the ring safely.

during the seven days. The three of them agreed to a place that they They considered it very safe. The ring was therefore kept there.

Unknown to the drummer, however, the bosses had contacted one of the two wives and bribed her with a large amount of money to bring them the ring. She collected the ring from the palace where it was hidden and gave it to the chiefs.

Immediately the ring entered her hands, they called some oarsmen from

canoe and entered the middle of the sea. They dropped the ring into the sea and

they returned home.

When the bosses were sure the ring could never be retrieved from the bottom

from the sea, they summoned the drum to return the ring to the palace the next day

for noon. The drummer went home confident that he would get the ring back.

simply from where it was hidden and return to the palace the next day. But

Alas, he searched everywhere, but he couldn't find the ring. He called his

two wives, but they couldn't find the ring. Therefore, he went to his

Babalawo.

The Bábálawo asked him to keep his mind at rest. He was

insured once

his Ori was still solidly behind him, No King could kill him. he

they asked him to offer a sacrifice of a large, freshly caught fish.

Hearing this, he hastened to the sea to weave a trap for the fish. The next day,

he returned to inspect his trap and found that he had already caught some fish big. What he did not know, however, was that Èsù Òdàrà had already guided the fish in the direction from where the ring was dropped, he made the fish to swallow the ring and at the same time guide the fish in the direction of the drum trap.

Drum hurried to Bàbáláwo's house with the fish. As soon as the fish was cut open in preparation for sacrifice, the ring was found inside his intestine of him. Drum was full of joy. Immediately after sacrifice, the Drum headed towards the King's palace.

In the King's palace, there was a crowd of people waiting to give

testimony of the drama that was to be revealed. The drum entered the palace and

there was complete silence. The chiefs asked him if he still believes that if the Orí of one will not kill one, no King can, and he answered in the affirmative. The bosses

They then asked the drummer to produce the King's ring. The drum went straight, diverting

to the chiefs and gave the King the ring. There was loud applause in the palace. The King and his

bosses were all put to shame.

The following week, the drummer was again summoned to the king's palace. It was

delivered ring again for safekeeping. He also returned home and narrated the story to his two wives. The three also agreed on where hide the ring The next day, one of the wives was bribed again and she she gave the ring to the bosses. The chiefs went to dig a path then hiding the ring inside the hole and plugging it down in a clever way. The day next, the drummer was summoned again and was asked to produce the ring on next noon. Drum returned home and found the lost ring. he called in his handcuffs, but they couldn't locate the ring. Then he came back again

new to his Bábálawo.

The Bàbáláwo assured him that he would overcome the tribulation. They asked him to go and get two hundred grasshoppers (locusts) whose holes were along the path. He left immediately on task. When he was doing this, Èsù Òdàrà directed his pay attention to taking the route by bosses. At the same time, Èsù Òdàrà made a grasshopper to dig its own hole in the same spot where the ring was buried. When he was about to dig out the 200 grasshoppers, he dug for outside the ring of Olofin together with the insect. He hastened to the house of Bàbáláwo.

After the sacrifice, he headed towards the king's house.

In the palace, the chiefs also asked him if he still believed in the statement of the oracle that he answered in the affirmative. They asked him to produce the ring and he he did. Once again, they put the King and the heads of him to shame.

The drum was summoned for the third time. The ring was still given back to him for

custody. He returned home with the ring; he informed the wives of it. They decided

where to keep the ring. The ring was saved. The treacherous wife was bribed still again and the ring was handed over to the chiefs. The chiefs went and buried the ring inside the dumpster. The next day drum was summoned and he was asked to bring the day after the ring. He got home, but he couldn't find it. He returned his Babalawo. The Awo asked him to offer the sacrifice of 200 worms chosen from the garbage collector. He set out on his assignment. The worm 200 that he was to pick was on

of Olofin's ring. He went to his Awo with the worms and

the ring. The sacrifice was

offered. The drum headed towards Olofin's palace with the ring.

At the palace, he wondered if he still believed the oracle's statement. He he replied that he believes it more than ever before. They asked him to produce the ring. He

he handed it over to Olofin. There was once again a loud ovation in the palace.

Olofin then declared that they convinced him that if one's Orí did not kill one, no King can kill the person. He divided his property in two and gave one part of it to the drum. He also made her a chief in his palace. The drum was so happy that he began to sing, dance and praise the Bábálawo of him like this:

Bí Irì eni kò pa'ni;
Obà kan kò leè pa'ni;
Díá fún Alundùndùn ilé Olófin;
Nigbàti nbè
nínú idààmu ayé;
Wón ní kó sákáalé, ebo ní síse;
Ó gbé'bo, Ó rúbo;
Kò pé, kó jìnnà
Iré gbogbo wá ya dé tùrtúru;
Èrò Ìpo, èrò Òfà;
Eyín ò mò wípé b'Orí eni ò pa'ni
Kò sí Oba tó leè pa'ni?

142

Translation:
If one's Ori didn't kill one
No king can kill one
This was the declaration of the Oracle to the drum of
Dùndún in the palace of Olofin
When he was faced with tribulations
They asked him to offer sacrifice
he fulfilled
Before a long time, not too far
All the Iré of life came in abundance
Travelers to Ipó and Òfá
Do not make it known that if the Orí of One does not kill
one
There is no King who can kill one
Ifá says that his Orí is fully supportive of him and that no
one can plan against you

and be successful. Ifá also warned a woman to never betray
her husband, unless she wants to expose herself to shame.
In the same way, no one should betray his friend, business
partner, club member and so on, to

that you don't have to be embarrassed. Also no one should
try to execute another

person because of his or her belief or conviction. If this is
done, Ifá will punish the

evil perpetrators and will cause the victim's triumph to fall
on them.

OGBE OSA VERSE 4

Owó ri iyán;
Owó suké;
Àtànpàràkò ri àgbàdo òjò;
Ó se mulunkú-mulùnkú;
Díá fún
Ogbè;
Tó nlo rè gbé omo rè sá g'òkè àjà;
Intori ikú;
Wón ní kó sákáalè, ebo ní síse
Ó gbébo, Ó rúbo

Translation:
The hand perceived the crushed yam
And she developed a hump
Her thumb saw the corn of the rainy season
And she moved back and forth (peeling the corn seed)
They were the ones who launched Ifá for Ogbè
Going to hide all his children inside the attic
due to death
They advised him to offer sacrifice
He complied.

PROPHESY

Ifá says that he foresees the Iré of longevity for you. Ifá says that, although death

is drawing near, you need to offer sacrifice in order to avert death imminent. You need to offer sacrifice in the attic or inside the roof of your house, while the ritual is also performed to Ifá. When this is done, the spirit evil that had been responsible for bringing death to your home will be rendered ineffective.

Pàtaki

Ogbè was having premonitions of disaster. So, he slept and he had a nightmare. He saw his children being taken away from him and led on the board of sacrifice. He therefore went to the Awo above for the Ifá consultation.

During the consultation, Ogbè-Òsá revealed himself.

The Awo Ogbè informed of the urgent need to offer sacrifice for him and all the members of his household save to ward off death from them. They asked him to

perform Ifá ritual with two fish, two rats, four kola nuts and money inside inside the attic of his house. He complied. They also asked him to get an empty gourd, bathing with ALUPAIDA leaves and Ogbè-Òsá impression on the Ìyèròsùn, pour it into the gourd and put the gourd in front of his house. He fulfilled.

When the ritual was going on inside the attic, Death, Grief, loss and Litigation they entered the house of Ogbè, they investigated all the rooms, but they did not They found no one in the house. They all left disappointed.

Moments later, Ogbè and his family came down from the attic. When he realized that

Death, Grief, Loss, and Litigation had all made unsuccessful
trips to his his house, he was full of joy, singing and dancing
thus:

Owó ri iyán;
Owó suké;
Àtànpàràkò ri àgbàdo òjò;
Ó se mulunkú-mulùnkú;
Díá fún Ogbè;
Tó nlo rè gbé omo rè sá g'òkè àjà;
Intori ikú;
Wón ní kó sákáalè, ebo ní síse Ó gbébo, Ó rúbo;
Njé ikú woléè mi kò bá mi;
Kèrègbè òfifo;
Ikú mà kú àrìndànù Àjà ni mo wà;
Ni mo ti n bo Ikin;
Arun woléè mi kò bá mi;
Kèrègbè òfifo;
Arun o mà kú Àrìndànù;
Àjà ni mo wà;
Ni mo ti n bo Ikin;
Òfò woléè mi kò bá mi;
Kèrègbè òfifo Òfò o mà kù àrìndànù;
Àjà ni mo wà;
Ni mo ti n bo Ikin;
Ejó woléè mi kò bá mi Kèrègbè òfifo;
Ejó o mà kù àrìndànù;
Àjà ni mo wà;
Ni mo ti n bo Ikin;
Gbogbo Irunbi í woléè mi won ò bá mi;
Kèrègbè òfifo;
Irunbi o mà kú àrìndànù;
Àjá ni mo wà Ni mo ti n bo Ikin;

146

Àpada ló ní kí gbogbo ibi ó padà léyìn mi.
  Translation:
The hand perceived the crushed yam
And she developed a hump
Her thumb saw the corn of the rainy season
And she moved back and forth (peeling the corn seed)
They were the ones who launched Ifá for Ogbè
Going to hide all his children inside the attic
due to death
They advised him to offer sacrifice
he fulfilled
Now, Death entered my house, but I was not found
This is it, but an empty pumpkin
Death afflicted by an unsuccessful journey
I was in the attic
Propitiating my Holy Grain
The afflictions entered my house, but they did not find me
This is it, but an empty pumpkin
affliction, afflicted by an unsuccessful journey
I was in the attic
Propitiating my Holy Grain
The loss entered my house, but I was not found
This is it, but an empty pumpkin
Loss, grieving for a fruitless journey
I was in the attic
Propitiating my Holy Grain
All the evil spirits entered my house, but they did not find
me
This is it, but an empty pumpkin
Evil spirits, afflicted for a fruitless journey
I was in the attic
Propitiating my Holy Grain
It was ÀPADÀ (àlúpàídà) those commands that all evils

147

must desist from

follow me

Ifá says that all evils will recede and you will live a long time

OGBE OSA VERSE 5

Ahóhóóhó, ahóyoyo;

Ayòyòòyò títí;

A k'áyò wolé;

Díá fún won ní Ìbejì agbáwójo

Wón ní ki won sákáalè, ebo ní síse

Translation:

We shout and rejoice

We rejoice without end

And brought happiness in our houses

They were ones who cast Ifá for them in the twins' house, where the

money is being accumulated

They were asked to offer sacrifice.

PROPHESY

Ifá says that it foresees the whole Iré of life for you. Ifá says that everything you needs to do to strengthen all the Iré of life, is to perform rituals to the deity of the twins (Ibeji).

Pàtaki

The people in the twins' house were finding it extremely difficult to

make meeting of final encounters. They had no money, no

husband, no

offspring and no bright future. Therefore, they approached the Awo above expressed for the consultation of Ifá.

They were advised to offer sacrifice with two guinea fowl, two pigeons and money. They were also asked to perform rituals to the deity of the Twins with sugar cane, beans, banana, rooster, assorted food, and money. At first, they they refused to comply. All they were doing did not yield any results fruitful.

When they realized in the future that there was no short cut to success except offer the sacrifice and perform the ritual, they returned to the Babalawo and did what he asked them to do. Since that time, those who had no money became wealthy, those without husbands had agreements, those without children They became proud parents. They were all singing and dancing and giving it praises to his Bábálawo who in turn was praising Òrúnmìlà like this:

Ahóhóóhó, ahóyoyo;
Ayòyòòyò títí;
A k'áyò wolé;
Díá fún won ní Ìbejì agbáwójo
Wón ní kó sákáalè, ebo ní síse;
Igbà ti e ò ké Ìbejì;
Òun le ò lájé;
Igbà ti e ò ké Ìbejì
Òun le ò l'áya;
Ìgbà tì e ò ké Ìbejì;
Òun le ò bí'mo;

Ìgbà ti e wá ké Ìbejì
Ni gbogbo Ire wolé.
  Translation:
We shout and rejoice
We rejoice without end
And brought happiness in our houses
They were the ones who cast Ifá for them at the twins'
house, where the
money is being accumulated
They were asked to offer sacrifice
When you did not propitiate the Deity of the Twins
you had no wealth
When you did not propitiate the Deity of the Twins
You did not guarantee the spouses
When you did not propitiate the Deity of the Twins
You did not father the children
But when we propitiate the Deity of the Twins now
All the good things of life came abundantly to us.
  Ifá says that you have a union or intimate relationship with
the Deity of the Twins.
You must make the appropriate propitiation so that your
success and other Iré will open up to you with ease.

OGBE OSA VERSE 6

Àròyé, Awo Àgbìgbò;
Díá fún Àgbìgbònìwònràn;
Tí wón ní ko ní lelà mó láíláí
Wón ní kó sákáalè, ebo ní síse;
Ó gbébo, Ó rúbo

150

Translation:
Talking endlessly, the Awo of Àgbìgbò (Hoopoe)
Ifá launch for the Àgbìgbònìwònràn (Hoopoe)
Who people said will never succeed in life
They advised him to offer sacrifice
He complied.

PROPHESY

Ifá says the client for whom this Odù is revealed he must always be telling Ifá

all his or her needs. Ifá says that so, doing, Ifá will do everything that he or

she needs for him or her.

Ifá says that you should always be telling Ifá all your needs. Ifá, he says that if he does it, Ifá will give you everything you need.

Ifá also says several people have written to you, but far from it, you I could never do anything to them in life. Ifá says that such people will be

embarrassed.

Pàtaki

Àgbìgbònìwònràn (Hoopoe) it was he who was experiencing hardship in his life of him He had no money, no house to live in, no wife, no children, no horse and no security of his next meal. everyone who we saw in rags, dirty and hungry concluded that he can never do it in his life of him Tired of this kind of life, he went to the Àròyé (speaking Endless) his Babaláwo for the consultation of Ifá. the Àròyé said Àgbìgbònìwònràn that he, Agbìgbò must always be narrating all his sufferings, his problems and penalties to Ifá. Àròyé told him that, for doing so, Ifá will take pity on him and give him all his needs in life. Agbìgbò was also said to never be cowardly or he was discouraged by the attitude of the people who are close to him. Agbigbò was informed that he was in the presence of the slander of him that he would become a succesful man. They asked him to offer sacrifice with two rats, two fish, one goat and money. He complied. He began to narrate all his problems to Ifá then.

Before long, Ifá began to bless him with all things so far blocked money with wife, children, house, horses and so on. He burst into tears of joy saying:

Àròyé, Awo Àgbìgbò;
Díá fún Àgbìgbònìwònràn;
Tí wón ní ko ní lelà mó láiĺáí Wón ní kó sákáalè, ebo ní síse;
Ó gbébo, Ó rúbo;
Aroye o dé o, Awo Agbìgbò Wón so wípé tèmi í tán;
Ifá ni tèmi í kù;
Àròyé o, Awo Agbìgbò
  Translation
Talking endlessly, the Awo of Àgbìgbò (Hoopoe)
I launch Ifá for the Àgbìgbònìwònràn (Hoopoe)
Who people would never succeed in life
They advised him to offer sacrifice

He complied.
Here comes Àròyé (talking endlessly) the Awo of Agbìgbò
They said mine is over
Ifá says that what is mine remains
All are hailed by Àròyé, the Awo of Agbìgbò,

Ifá says that such people will be put to shame. Ifá says that
its slanderers they will suffer shame. And this will be in your
very presence and you will become one very important
personality. All you need to do is follow telling your
problems to Ifá regularly without extremes and everything
that you missing Ifá will provide it.

OGBE OSA VERSE 7

Ogójì ni wón fi n kó'fá Ogbè'Sá;
Díá fún Mo-rádáró-mi-ò-rálé;
Wón ní kó sákáalè, ebo
ní síse;
Ó gbébo, Ó rúbo.

Translation:
It has 40 (cowries) that people use to offer Ogbè'Sá sacrifice
That was Ifá's statement to "I-only-see-morning-but-can't-
see-night"
They asked him to offer sacrifice
He complied.

PROPHESY

Ifá says that you should think more about your future than
about the past or present. Yes, you have any problem now,

you must think that the future will be Pink for you.

On the other hand, if you have been successful in the past and present, you should be cautious. in the future. You should not think that the situation will continue to be the same forever. Also, you should never make fun of those conditions, no they are favorable presently because you do not know what may happen in the future.

Reciprocally, no one should joke with you because the situation is not favorable at present, as no one knows what the future has in store for you.

Pàtaki

Mo-rádárò-mi-ò-rálé (I-only-see-tomorrow-but-cannot-see-night, in other words, this is the present I see, but I cannot determine what the future Will it will seem) went to his Babaláwo when his situation was very pathetic. your companions they were making fun of him because of his failure in almost every facet of life. The Babaláwo assured him, however, that his future will be rewarded. They asked him to offer sacrifice with 40 cowries shelled the same day he consulted Ifá.

He is also asked to later come and offer sacrifice with two guinea-fowl, two chickens and money. He complied.

Before long, the achievement gate opened for him while many of his companions who were making a joke of him came to him with cap in hand and started to favors from him. He was in favor so full of gratitude to Olodumare for the turn of events.

Ogójì ni wón fi n kó'fá Ogbè'Sá;
Díá fún Mo-rádárò-mi-ò-rálé;
Wón ní kó sákáalè, ebo ní síse;
Ó gbébo, Ó rúbo;
Èyin ti e rí Àárò;
E rora se o;
Èyin ti e rí Àárò;
E ò r'Álé
Èyin ti e rí Àárò;
E rora se o
  Translation:
It has 40 (cowries) that people use to offer Ogbè'Sá sacrifice
That was Ifá's statement to "I-only-see-morning-but-can't-see-night"
They asked him to offer sacrifice
He complied.
Those who see this morning (today)
Be very careful
those who see this morning
You don't see the night (future)
those who see this morning
Be very careful
Ifá says that an adequate provision must be constituted in the future for you, if the situation is unfavourable. On the other hand, you should not lose hope. If he presents is unfavourable.

OGBE OSA VERSE 8

Ó ró wen;

Ó dà wen;
B'óníde bá se rìn;
Béè ni'de rè n dun;
A f'ìjà gb'èrù;
Awo ilé
Àlàpà;
Díá fún Àlàpà;
Ó n f'ekun sùngbérè Ire gbogbo
  Translation:
It had a metallic sound
It had a resonant metallic sound
Way to staff which was decorated with brass (copper) rides
So too will your resonant clang brass ornament
He who collects material sacrifices by force
The resident Awo of Àlàpà
He was the one who launched Ifá for the Àlàpà
Crying in lament at his inability to have any Ire of life
PROPHESY

Ifá says that he foresees an Iré for you. Ifá also says that you do not have money in the time to consult the Oracle, but you must look for six units of money, for that situation and must give it to the Awo who launched the Odù that same day. because your success is in your hands. You should not risk your opportunities by not giving him the money to the Babaláwo. After this, you must perform ritual to Òshùn. This

Deity will be the instrument for the achievement of your success.

Pàtaki

The only thing that Àlàpà could, was the fact that he was the King of Apa. What's more,

that, there was nothing to show in terms of achievement; he didn't have any money,

no presentable dress befitting Obà's high-ranking hierarchy, no wife, no children, no horse and no good prestige in the Oba community. He therefore called in his Awo for Ifá consultation.

During the consultation, Ogbè - 'Sá was revealed. The Babaláwo informed him that his

poverty was over the same day and then he performs ritual to Òsùn with 10 chickens

fresh egg, 10 fresh bananas, a chicken and money. Àlàpà were of agreed to offer the sacrifice and perform the ritual, but said that he had no money with than him to get hold of the material at that time.

Afijà gbèrù (the Babaláwo of Àlàpà) I don't take that. He insisted that Àlàpà must get the money immediately and that his time was not to be wasted. Àlàpà appeal to him to see reason with him (Àlàpà) that, if there was money, he would share it happily

for sacrifice. Afijà gbèrù simply grabbed Àlàpà and continued to fight. When Àlàpà was able to free himself

157

from Afijà gbèrù's hold, he took to his heels and Afijà-gbèrù followed him in hot pursuit.

It was then that they met Òsùn by the river bank. She adorned herself with brass ornaments; she had brass bangles on her neck, hands and legs.

When she moved, the bangles made the same rhythmic sound as hers accompanied hers.

Àlàpà ran to her and looking for protection. Afijà-gbèrù insisted that Àlàpà must pay

the six units or money before he was released. Therefore, she asked

the two narrate her stories to her.

Àlàpà said that he consulted Ifá because he had nothing in his life in the way of achievement.

The Babaláwo advised him to offer sacrifice with six units of money that he I did not have. He also told him (Àlàpà) to perform ritual to Òsùn. Àlàpà said that he was prepared to do all these things, but there was no money to do them. Alapa was that the depression beyond his life, he had never heard of it for a while when any Babaláwo insisted on taking the sacrificial materials from his customers through force. He concluded that if he had known that such a way, he would never have ventured to ask the Babaláwo to consult Ifá to he; he wanted only to solve a problem to end up adding another.

Afijà-gbèrù said that when he consulted Ifá for the Àlàpà, Ifá said that all his Trouble would be up that day. Àlàpà must offer the six units of money that day in front of the poverty of him will disappear. Afijà-gbèrù maintained that he was in the best interest of the client to seek the money by all means so that their problems disappeared. Afijà-gbèrù then concluded that he was not prepared leave Àlàpà unless and until he found the money for the sacrifice that day.

Osun then asked Afijà-gbèrù if it was possible for her to pay the money for Àlàpà. Afijà-gbèrù answered in the affirmative. Osun then gave him the money. There and then the sacrifice was made for the Àlàpà by the side of the road. Both of them They returned to their respective homes.

Three days after Àlàpà performed the sacrifice, all the small towns that surround his town, they had decided to come and pay his respects and taxes. They they came with money, food, clothes, horses and many marks of respect and friendship. He was very pleased. He thus quickly summoned Afijà-gbèrù to his from her palace the ritual to Osun could be performed immediately. After this he erected a grove of osun at this place and regularly performed rituals to osun. Alapa he also made the Principal Babaláwo of him to Afijà-gbèrù and showered him with gifts.

Ó ró wen;
Ó dà wen;
B'óníde bá se rìn;
Béè ni'de rè n dun;

159

A f'ìjà gb'èrù;
Awo ilé Àlàpà;
Díá fún Àlàpà;
Ó n f'ekun sùngbérè Ire gbogbo;
Wón ní kó sákáalè, ebo ní Síse;
Ó gbébo, Ó rúbo;
Kò pé, ko jìnnà;
Ire gbogbo wá ya dé tùrtúru
Translation:
It had a metallic sound
Possessed a resonant metallic sound
Way to staff which was decorated with brass (copper) rides
So too will your resonant clang brass ornament
He who collects material sacrifices by force
The resident Awo of Àlàpà
He was the one who launched Ifá for Àlàpà
Crying in lament at his inability to have any life IRE
They advised him to offer sacrifice
he fulfilled
Before long, not too far
All the Iré of life came in abundance.

Ifá says that all his sufferings will become a thing of the past. You must not without
However, forget about those who helped you achieve success.

OGBE OSA VERSE 9

Ebi n pa inú ù mi ihálá-ihálá;
Ebi n pa inú ù mi ihàlà-ihàlà;
Ebi n pa inú ù mi ihàlà-Ihòlo;
Díá fún Àrìkúlolá;

160

Omo ayàn'kàrà mògùrò lale Ifè

Translation:
My hunger is very severe
My hunger is almost unbearable
My hunger is serious, for my stomach to be empty
He launched Ifá for Àrìkúlolá
He who bought fried bean cakes to consume palm wine raffia in Ile-
Ifè

PROPHESY

Ifá says that he foresees an Iré of wealth for you. Ifá says that you will have a lot success in your business. You will also be very popular far and wide. Ifá warns, however, that you should not be leaving your stomach empty. You should never fast for any social or religious purpose to prevent a bowel problem.

His wealth is now almost in his hands. You must offer sacrifice and you must perform ritual to Ifá.

Pàtaki

Àrìkúlolá wanted to know if he would be a very successful man in his life. He also they said what he must do to achieve that success. He therefore went to the Awo above expressed by the consultation of Ifá.

Àrìkúlolá was informed that he would be a very successful

man in his life. As well told him that he does not need to save the money he has to spend on food before that he became a wealthy person. They told him that he was eating regularly and that his riches will come whether he eats regularly or not. he was without however better for him to eat regularly so that when wealth came, he would not was spending to find a remedy to offer sacrifice with a dove, a guinea fowl and money. After this, he went to perform Ifá ritual with akara (fried bean cakes) and Ògùrò (raffia palm wine). He complied.

Ebi n pa inú ù mi ihálá-ihálá;
Ebi n pa inú ù mi ihàlà-ihàlà;
Ebi n pa inú ù mi ihàlà-Ihòlo;
Díá fún Àrìkúlolá;
Omo ayàn'kàrà mògùrò lale Ifè;
Wón ní kó sákáalè, ebo ní Síse;
Ó gbébo, Ó rúbo;
Njé kinni yóó fa're ilè yìí wá fún wa o? ;
Ògùrò;
Ni yóó fa Ire ilè yìí wá fún wa;
Ògùrò;
Ire Ajé Onífè kó dìde wá bá wa;
Ògùrò;
Ni yóó fa Ire ilè yìí
wá fún wa o;
Ògùrò
 Translation:
My hunger is very severe
My hunger is almost unbearable
My hunger is serious, for my stomach is empty

The Ifá launch for Àrìkúlolá
He who bought fried bean cakes to consume raffa palm wine
in Ile-Ifè
They advised him to offer sacrifice
he fulfilled
I pray, that it will drag the Ire of this land to us
Ògùrò (raffia palm wine)
It is he that will drag the IRE of this land to us
Oguro
He allows the Ilé-Ifè rising wealth IRE and comes to us
Oguro
It is I who will drag the IRE of this land to us
Oguro
Ifá says that the client will have many opportunities to
succeed. However the You should make good use of these
opportunities.

OGBE OSA VERSE 10

Ohun tí se Babaláwo;
Bí kó bá tán;
Àwon Ològbèrì;
Won a kenu bò'kòkò;
Won a ke'enu bò'bábá;
Wón á máa rín èrín i rè wúyéwúyé;
Díá fún Òrúnmìlà;
Baba jí, Baba
bá Irunbi o;
Wón ní kí Baba sákáalè, ebo ní síse o;
Ó gbébo, Ó rúbo

Translation:
The problems faced by a Bàbáláwo
163

If not completely resolve in time
The ignorant, uninitiated ones
Put your mouth in corners
Put their mouths in cracks
The will is laughing at Bàbáláwo's misfortune in secret
These were Ifá's declaration to Òrúnmìlà
When he woke up and was confronted with evil forces
They advised him to offer sacrifice
He complied.

PROPHESY

Ifá says that he foresees an Iré of long life and Iré of victory over all the forces bad against you. Ifá says that you had been experiencing problems with these evil forces for quite some time. Ifá says that it is now time for these forces to leave you, so that those who were ignorant of your real problems stop making fun of you. Ifá says that you must offer the sacrifice and the bad forces will flee from his side.

Pàtaki

Òrúnmìlà was confronting himself with the problems of death, afflictions, litigation and loss. He tried all he could to disperse them but the Problem kept repeating itself. Therefore, he went to his students for the Ifá consultation.

Òrúnmìlà was told that he could solve his problem. he was sure too that those who had been jubilant that as great as Òrúnmìlà was, he he found it difficult to solve his own problem will he be silenced. orunmila was asked to offer sacrifice with matured male goat, ègbèsì leaves and money.

He fulfilled. The leaves spread out inside the sacrificial vessel as everyone the other sacrificial materials were placed on top of the leaves. The container was put then where Ifá prescribed for Òrúnmìlà.

Behind the sacrifice, Èsù-Òdàrà came to the house of Òrúnmìlà and scattered all the bad forces. That was how Òrúnmìlà was able to conquer the evil forces that give him problems. He was full of joy and gratitude to Olódùmarè. He was singing dancing and saying:

Ohun tí se Babaláwo;
Bí kó bá tán;
Àwon Ològbèrì;
Won a kenu bò'kòkò;
Won a ke'enu bò'bábá;
Wón á máa rín èrín i rè wúyéwúyé;
Díá fún Òrúnmìlà;
Baba jí, Baba bá Irunbi o;
Wón ní kí Baba sákáalè, ebo ní síse o;
Ó gbébo, Ó rúbo;
Njé ikú máa lo o;
Arun máa lo;
Ejó maa lo;
Òfò máa lo;
Ègbèsì oko;
Gbogbo irunbi e mà tóó deyin

Translation:
The problems faced by a Babaláwo
If not fully resolved in time
The ignorant, uninitiated ones

165

Put your mouth in corners
Put their mouths in cracks
The will is laughing at Babaláwo's misfortune in secret
These were the declaration of Ifá to the Òrúnmìlà
When he woke up and was confronted with evil forces
They advised him to offer sacrifice
He complied.
Now death is gone
the affliction goes away
litigation goes away
losses go away
Ègbèsì leaves the farm
All evil forces is supreme time you all take away (from me)
Ifá says that all evil spirits will disappear from your life.

OGBE OSA VERSE 11

Aféfé lélé níí sawo Ìsálú Ayé;
Èfúùfù lèlè níí sawo Ìsálú Òde Òrún;
Kùkùte kùkùùkù,
Awo èbá ònà;
Ògan yo lòòlò Jana, Awo eséko;
Díá fún Ìkì;
Tíí sòré Àgbò-mìnìnjò
  Translation:
The gentle breeze is the Awo of the Earth
The gentle wind is the Awo of the Heavens
The short heavy trunk is that the Awo of the road are next
to
Ogan vines that creep along the road, the Awo of the farm,
They were the ones who launched Ifá for Ìkì
Who is a close friend of Àgbò-mìnìnjò

PROPHESY

Ifá says that this client should be careful of friends. You must not follow no friend to go out without first telling those who are close to you your whereabouts, the identity of your partner and the length of your stay outside the House.

The you should also propitiate your parental ancestral spirit with a ram. The spirit of your ancestor is solidly behind you, Ifá also says that you must not betray your accomplished friends; you must not betray your friend or betray the trust placed in you. You shouldn't plan anything bad for her friends, so that the nemesis does not reach her (just punishment).

Pàtaki

Ìkì and Àgbò-mìnìnjò were close friends. They were almost inseparable. They usually went everywhere together. Wherever Ìkì was found, Ìkì was certainly nearby. The two were so close that they became the benchmark of how true friends should be among their community.

One day, Ìkì slept and they were sleepy. He saw himself sinking into a deep well. On

place of water covering his body, he discovered that he was covered with blood. He

he also discovered the mortification he endured was split open while his his intestines were dragging along the path. Immediately he He woke up and went directly to the

Babaláwo mentioned above for the Ifá consultation.

The Babaláwo asked him to be careful about answering any calls from the backyard. He was also warned against ever following anyone anywhere. The Babaláwo told him that he is in grave danger from those he considered to be his close friends of his. Therefore, they advised him to offer sacrifice with a ram and perform ritual to the spirit of his paternal ancestor with another ram. He complied.

A few days later, his friend Àgbò-mìnìnjò came to his house in the afternoon. He yelled the name of Ìkì from the backyard. Although Ìkì remembered that he had been warned against answering any calls from his backyard, he reasoned that such warning could not include Àgbò-mìnìnjò who all the wise world was his best friend of his. Àgbò-mìnìnjò told Ìkì that he would like Ìkì to accompany a cause important. Ìkì remembered that they had asked him not to follow anyone at any part someday, but he also thought that such a warning was not posible include Àgbò-mìnìnjò his best friend. Therefore, Ìkì agreed to follow Àgbò-mìnìnjò. While they were following the path, Àgbò-mìnìnjò he seized Ìkì energetically, they threw him into a sack and he tied the sack hermetically.

Unknown to Ìkì however, Àgbò-mìnìnjò had always been envious of the achievements of Ìkì. He considered Ìkì a threat to his own success. Àgbò-mìnìnjò couldn't see the reason why we would all be talking about two successful friends and not from Àgbò-mìnìnjò a successful man. In

168

other words, Àgbò-mìnìnjò wanted to have success exclusively and not be compared to his friend. Also unknown to Ìkì, Olofin wanted to perform a ritual to the spirits of his ancestors. The Babaláwo asked Olofin to bring an animal for the ritual. Olofin was on the verge of securing one when Àgbò-mìnìnjò entered his (Olofin) palace. He asked Olofin so that he he was watching and Olofin told him. Àgbò-mìnìnjò told Olofin to prepare all the other ritual materials ready when he was going to present Olofin with the animal that, Olofin, would use to propitiate his ancestors. Olofin was full of gratitude to Àgbò-mìnìnjò. After ligating the sack tightly, he carried the bundle in his head. Ìkì thought it was a joke. He therefore asked Àgbò-mìnìnjò what it was all about a joke. It was then that Àgbò-mìnìnjò told Ìkì how he he had been feeling from the beginning. Àgbò-mìnìnjò concluded by saying to Ìkì that Ìkì was going to be taken to Olofin's palace to be used in the execution of the ritual for the propitiation of the ancestors of Olofin.

That was finally the time it dawned on Ìkì that he was in serious danger. He appealed to Àgbò-mìnìnjò please spare his life, but all his plea fell on deaf ears. When he made those pleas, they did not work and he is only a few moments at the time of this death, he remembered that the Awo who consulted Ifá for he had told her about being wary of this that they asked to be friends with him. He he also remembered that he had trusted his captor implicitly before for him to follow him out. Not knowing that to do it later, he called in all his Awo for help while doing this, he made a howl at her wail of a scream, he made the dirge of him (ìyèrè), the dirge of lament and said:

Béè nì o o;
Aféfé lélé níí sawo Ìsálú Ayé .o. Èfùfù lèlè níí sawo Ìsálú Òde
Òrún o Kùkùte kùkùùkù, Awo èbá ònà o;
Ògún yo lòòlò Jana, Awo eséko o;
Díá fún Ìkì tíí sòré Àgbò-mìnìnjò o;
Día f'Àgbò-mìnìnjò ti n gbé Ìkì lo bá Olófin;
Èfùfù lèlè sáré wá o wá gbà mì lówó asebi o héè;
Èfùfù lèlè sáré wá o wá gbà mì lówó asebi;
Èfùfù lèlè sáré wá o wá gbà mì lówó asebi

Translation:
The gentle breeze is the Awo of the Earth
The gentle wind is the Awo of the Heavens
under heavy bad smell, the Awo of the roadside
Ogan vines that creep along the road, the Awo of the farm,
You were the ones who launched Ifá for Ìkì who was the friend of Àgbò-mìnìnjò

You also launched Ifá for Àgbò-mìnìnjò who was taking Ìkì to the house of Olofin (to be killed) Gentle breeze please rush here and rescue me from a bad person Pray the Gentle Breeze please hurry here rescue me from a bad person I beg, the Gentle Breeze please hurry here rescue me from a person bad Immediately after this, the gentle breeze from the land combined with the mind sky and created a heavy storm. They moved the dust and particles from the dust entered them the eyes of Àgbò-mìnìnjò. He began to

170

stagger.

While he was doing this, he got his legs entangled in Ogan's vine and the thorns tore at his leg. While he was trying to untangle himself, he she pressed his body against the bad smell by the side of the road. Your perception of load by the side of the road.

Immediately after this, the spirit of Ìkì's paternal ancestors that he had propitiated earlier descended and untied the rope with which the sack was tied. Ìkì escaped. The hereditary spirit replaced Ìkì with a lump of grass by the side of the road and tied it behind.

When Àgbò-mìnìnjò was finally enabled to command, he carried his load simply and rush to the palace of Olofin. He felt that he had lost too long on the way and he couldn't afford to spend any more time inspecting his cargo.

When Àgbò-mìnìnjò arrived at the palace, all the other ritual materials were ready and the Babaláwo just proceeded with the ritual. when it was time to use to Ìkì to finish the ritual procedure, they asked Àgbò-mìnìnjò unleash the load from him and bring the gift from him. When the sack was untied, they discovered that it was just a lump of grass that was inside the sack. Nobody waited for Àgbò-mìnìnjò to explain himself before he was caught and propitiated the spirits hereditary of Olofin. From that day, Olofin decreed that a ram must be used hereafter as ritual material to propitiate his ancestors.

171

That was how Ìkì was able to overcome the bad plans of his friend. he was so happy that he decided to rè-offer the sacrifice. They told him, however, that the people do not offer sacrifice twice in the same Odù for the same purpose. All he needed to do was give praise to his Awo who will give praise to his once to the Òrúnmìlà. Òrúnmìlà will then give thanks to Olódùmarè.

Aféfé lélé níí sawo Ìsálú Ayé.o. Èfùfù lèlè níí sawo Ìsálú
Òde Òrún o;
Kùkùte kùkùùkù, Awo èbá ònà o;
Ògún yo lòòlò Jana, Awo eséko o;
Díá fún Ìkì tíí sòré Àgbò-mìnìnjò o;
Día f'Àgbò-mìnìnjò ti n gbé Ìkì lo bá Olófin;
Wón ní kó sákáalè, ebo ní síse;
Ó gbébo, Ó rúbo;
Eyín ò rí Àgbò-mìnìnjò;
Ti n gbé ikò lo bá Olófin; Kò pé, kò jìnnà;
E wá bá ni láruúsé ogun
Translation:
The gentle breeze is the Awo of the Earth
The gentle wind is the Awo of the Heavens
under heavy bad smell, the Awo of the roadside
Ogan vines that creep along the road, the Awo of the farm,
You were one who launched Ifá for Ìkì who was the friend
of Àgbò-mìnìnjò
You also launched Ifá for Àgbò-mìnìnjò who was taking Ìkì
to the house of
Olofin
Not done that you see Àgbò-mìnìnjò
Who was taking Ìkì to Olofin's house
Before long, not too far

Look at us where we are accustomed to sacrifice to overcome the adversary

Ifá says that you should be careful with those who ask to be your friends. Ifá

It says that you could overcome your enemies.

OGBE OSA VERSE 12

Tanbélégé, Awo Ológéè-Òrìsà; Díá fún Ológéè-Òrìsà; Ológéè n menu sùnráhùn

t'omo

Translation:

Tanbélégé, is the Awo of Ológéè-Òrìsà

He was the one who launched Ifá for Ológéè-Òrìsà

When she was crying in lament for her childlessness

PROPHESY

Ifá says that the client must offer sacrifice against litigation. Ifá says that if the customer had collected something from someone to help save it, you should go and You must return that thing immediately. That is to prevent a serious problem.

Ifá also says that there is a barren woman with a horrible need to have a child, she must offer sacrifice. She will get pregnant. She must also do ritual to Òrìsànlá and Èshù.

Pàtaki

Ológéè-Òrìsà was a barren woman. She did all she knew to get pregnant to no avail. She therefore went to Tanbélégé for her Ifá consultation.

Tanbélégé told her that she would definitely get pregnant and have children. She asked to offer sacrifice with two rats, two fish, a goat and money. she fulfilled the same day. She was also asked to perform ritual to the Òrìsànlá with odun (red) cloth, 10 native chalks, 10 snails, cocoa butter, a rooster and money. She was Likewise, to perform a ritual to Èsù with a rooster, palm oil and money. She went to house to prepare for the rituals.

Tanbélégé Awo Òrìsà;
Díá fún Òrìsà;
Wón ní kó rúbo nítorí Ejó

Translation:
Tanbélégé, is the Awo of Òrìsà
He was the one who launched Ifá for the Òrìsà
Òrìsà was asked to offer sacrifice due to litigation
Òrìsà went to Tanbélégé to determine how his life will progress. they told him without
However, he was careful with litigation. They asked him not to keep custody of any property for the person. They also asked him to offer sacrifice with a rooster, a hen and money. Òrìsànlá refuscd to comply.

When Èsù Òdàrà learned that Òrìsànlá had not complied with the advice of the Babaláwo, he went to Òrìsànlá's house and asked him to help him by keeping cloth from Odùn.

174

Òrìsànlá agreed to save the cloth for Èsù. unknown to Obàtálá, Èsù had sneaked out inside Obàtálá's house and had reclaimed the fabric. The next day, Èsù Òdàrà returned to Obàtálá`s house to demand his cloth from Odùn. Obàtálá investigated everywhere, but could not find the cloth. Èsù Òdàrà accused Obàtálá of diverting the cloth from him for Obàtálá's personal use then. He said that Obàtálá deliberately stole the cloth from him and should be charged for it.

woo Òkè-Ìgètí. Èsù Òdàrà asked Obàtálá to kneel down. Obàtálá did.

Obàtálá sank Èsù Òdàrà then mounted Obàtálá's shoulder and Obàtálá order to take him (Èsù) to Òkè-Ìgètí. Obàtálá did. In the Òkè-Ìgètí mode, they they found Ológéè-Òrìsà with all the materials that they had asked him to he will buy to propitiate Obàtálá and Èsù Òdàrà. She asked Obàtálá why he he was dishonoring himself in this way. Obàtálá replied that he lost the cloth Odùn given to him by Èsù Òdàrà. Realizing that he had been asked before he will buy a cloth of Odùn for Tanbélégé (which she had already bought), Ológéè-Òrìsà told Obàtálá that the cloth was given to her by Obàtálá. She took out the cloth and she delivered Èsù Òdàrà. Obàtálá was surprised and relieved because he knew that he he had never given any cloth to Ológéè-Òrìsà and that it was just a tour to rid him of his present problem. When Èsù Òdàrà recovered the cloth; he demanded for a rooster, palm oil and money that were quickly given to him by Ológéè-Òrìsà.

Èsù Òdàrà then jumped down from Obàtálá's shoulders and continued on his way.

Obàtálá asked Ológéè-Òrìsà that she was really looking at him. she told Obàtálá that she was barren and they had asked her to perform a ritual for Obàtálá to that he the womb would open to give birth to a child. Obàtálá prayed for her and she left.

The following month, she became pregnant and she delivered many children afterwards, she was full of joy and happiness until she died.

Tanbélégé, Awo Ológéè-Òrìsà;
Díá fún Ológéè-Òrìsà;
Ológéè n menu sùnráhùn t'omo Tanbélégé Awo Òrìsà;
Díá fún Òrìsà;
Wón ní kó rúbo nítorí Ejó;
Kò pé, kò jìnà
E wá bá ni ní jèbútú omo

Translation:
Tanbélégé, is the Awo of Ológéè-Òrìsà
He was the one who launched Ifá for Ológéè-Òrìsà
When she was crying in lament for her missing child
Tanbélégé, is the Awo of Òrìsà
He was the one who launched Ifá for the Òrìsà
Òrìsà was asked to offer sacrifice due to litigation
Before long, not too far
Find us in the midst of many children

Ifá says that the client will be able to achieve the desire of her heart.

OGBE OSA VERSE 13

Ogbè sá re'lé;
Òsá sá r'oko;
Díá fún Eni-Ayé-kàn;
A bù fún séere

Translation:
Ogbè executed house
Òsá ran to the farm
They were ones who launched for the He-who-is-this-again-to-rule-the-world
They also launched Ifá to Do-it-good.

PROPHESY

Ifá says that an old sick person needs to offer sacrifice urgently to

survive the disease. Ifá says that the sick person is already preparing the

way for others to fill the void you are about to create as a result of your death. Ifá also says that those in positions of authority or command must govern well, so that at the same time people know their own benefits under their authority. All positions are temporary.

Pàtaki

An older man was very ill. The relationship of the man then took him to the two Awo mentioned above for the consultation of Ifá. They wanted to determine their chances of surviving the disease. They were told that the man had a very slim chance of survival but that whoever he was that would walk in the man's shoes must handle people's affairs well. They were advised to offer sacrifice of a ram that they never bothered to offer sacrifice. The man died shortly after.

Ogbè sá re'lé;
Òsá sá r'oko;
Díá fún Eni-Ayé-kàn;
A bù fún séere;
Séere o séere
Eni-Ayé-kàn;
E s'Ayé Ire;
Bó jé ìwo l'Ayé kàn;
Ko sayé ire o;
Bó jé èmi l'Ayé kàn
Ma s'ayé ire;
Séere o séere;
Eni-Ayé-kàn;
E s'ayé Ire

Translation:
Ogbè executed house
Òsá ran to the farm
They were ones who launched for the He-who-is-this-again-to-rule-the-world
They also launched Ifá to Do-it-good.

Pray, get it right, get it right
Those whose spin is he rule the word
to the good word
If this is the word rule again
Please rule the world well
If this is my word again govern
I will rule the world well
Get it right, get it right
If this is your word govern again
Please rule the world well

Ifá says that those in positions of authority should manage with consideration. Any position or authority is temporary (provisional).

OGBE OSA VERSE 14

Àháàrá-màjá;
Àwon araa won ni won n já araa won;
Díá fún Òrúnmìlà; Ifá n lo rèé
f'ojú kan Ikú Ayé;
Wón ní kó sákáalè, ebo ní síse;
Ó gbébo, Ó rúbo
  Traducción
Àháàrámàjá
They were one of them died
This was Ifá's declaration to Òrúnmìlà
When he was going to examine the unnatural cause of death
They advised him to offer sacrifice
He complied.
PROPHESY

Ifá says that you must offer sacrifice for an avoidable death.
Ifá says that most of the deaths that kill human beings are

not natural. In fact, Ifá says that all the deaths that kill the human being have their root in this world and not in heaven. Therefore, Ifá says that you must be extremely careful not to fall victim to any of the unnatural deaths.

Pàtaki

Òrúnmìlà discovered so many people were dying at their tender age. He discovered several deaths from poisoning, disease, drowning, suicide, bad opponent plans, accidents and so on. He decided to go and find out what the causes of these unnatural deaths then. For this reason, he went for Ifá consultation. He wanted to know if it was possible for him to know the root cause of unnatural death that kills the human being. They told him he would see the cause and that there was no death in heaven and death was here on earth. They asked him to offer sacrifice of three ripened goats so that he could use the goats to propitiate Ifá. He complied. He started to observe human activities then.

While observing him, he discovered that all human deaths were caused through four main factors: ignorance, stupidity, carelessness or obstinacy. He discovered that if human beings could avoid all these factors of untimely death, they would stay on the ground for a long time.

Àháàrá-màjá;
Àwon araa won ni won n já araa won;
Díá fún Òrúnmìlà;
Ifá n lo rèé
f'ojú kan Ikú Ayé;

Wón ní kó sákáalè, ebo ní síse;
Ó gbébo, Ó rúbo;
Kò sí Ikú kan
l'Òrun;
Ayé ni Ikú wà

Translation
Àháàrá-màjá
They were one of them died
This was Ifá's declaration to Òrúnmìlà
When he was going to examine the unnatural cause of death
They advised him to offer sacrifice
He complied.
There is no death in heaven
Death is here on earth.

Ifá says that we should try to avoid falling into ignorance,
stupidity, carelessness and obstinacy (stubbornness). They
are the four factors responsible for early deaths on Earth.

OGBE OSA VERSE 15

A gbó sáá-sáá má sàá;
A gbó yàà-yàà má yà;
A gbó kukúù má wòye;
Eye tí n je'ko
Díá fún Egbére;
Ti yóó se aya Òrúnmìlà
  Traducción:
She who was warned to run but refused to run
She who was warned to branch out and hide, but refused to
do so
The bird that kisses the farm lawn
These were the declaration of Ifá to EGBÉRE

181

Who will become the wife of Òrúnmìlà.

PROPHESY

Ifá says that there is a scarce woman (short, short, small)
where this Odù is revealed, who should be warned against
being too reckless and stubborn. She should be advised look
at her attitudes, because it will be very difficult for her to get
anyone who tolerates ser as a wife. She too must be warned
again, of the incessant scolding, endless crying and
complaining against her husband and her family.

Ifá also says that for a willing man to get married to a man
who out, or born by this Odù, he must be warned to marry
a woman scarce, the relationship as such will never become
a successful marriage. The woman she would scold,
complain and cry against her husband, and the extent of
their relationship they would get to the point that they would
send her to pack so that she leaves her house matrimonial.
Nothing and no one can satisfy her.

Pàtaki

Egbére saw Òrúnmìlà and liked him instantly. She planned
to become his wife for consequent. She went to some Awo
for Ifá consultation. They asked her to look her behavior if
she thinks to stay in any man's house. she told him advised
that she learn how to appreciate other people's efforts and
know adjust to any given situation. They told him that those
were the keys to have a successful material relationship.

They then advised him to offer sacrifice with a goat and the mat on which she slept. She abused the Babaláwo, calling them thief, that she told them that she would not change her attitude and she would not offer any sacrifice. She then made about her fixed goal of spoiling Òrúnmìlà with determination. Shortly after, she became the wife of Òrúnmìlà. As soon as she had entered the house of Òrúnmìlà that she began to complain against everyone and everything. She complained against Òrúnmìlà, his relationship, his work, his house, his clothes, her friends. She insisted that Òrúnmìlà should change everything that he had in her house, he agreed. But she began to complain against the new games of things she selected for Òrúnmìlà. She said Òrúnmìlà afterwards that he must annul His or her friends and family would have to pack away. Òrúnmìlà refused to comply.

Out of annoyance, she packed herself up and moved from one matrimonial home to another endlessly.

A gbó sáá-sáá má sàá;
A gbó yàà-yàà má yà;
A gbó kukúù má wòye;
Eye tí n je'ko
Díá fún Egbére;
Ti yóó se aya Òrúnmìlà;
Òrúnmìlà ló di Ògìrì -Ìyàndà;
Ifá jé ki ng ní
ibùjoòó ire;
Njé Egbére n lo lóhùn-ún araa re loni ò;
Egbére o

183

Translation:
She who was warned to run, but left refused to run
She who was warned to branch out and hide, but refused to
do so
The bird that kisses the farm lawn
These were the declaration of Ifá to Egbére
Who will become the wife of Òrúnmìlà.
Òrúnmìlà says that she has become ÒGÌRÌ-ÌYÀNDÀ now
Ifá please let me have a stable house
Egbére is following her foolish journey now
Egbere, what a shame
  Ifá says in this Odu, that the scarce woman must learn
marriage manners and

the simple rules of coexistence to enjoy a peaceful married
life.

OGBE OSA VERSE 16

Ikú won o d'ójó;
Àwon Àrùn won ò d'Ósù;
Díá fún Motóógbé;
Tíí s'omo Oníkàá

Translation:
Death never notifies
Afflictions never notify
These were Ifá's statement to Motóógbé
(I am quite prepared for marriage)
who was the daughter of Oníkàá.

PROPHESY

Ifá also says that there is a single woman where this Odù is revealed. if it were for

marriage, the woman must be made to go to the house of a man within seven days of

this Ifá revelation. This is due to the woman's life. She is a woman of Elegbe. If she does not go before that time, her heavenly husband will come and take her away.

will take and she will die.

Pàtaki

Motóógbé was having nightmares. She consulted Ifá accordingly to find out why. She wondered and informed her parents that she must surrender to her applicant within seven days of this revelation. They told him that if this were not done, she would die. She was however aware that she was an Elégbé

When she told her parents, they quickly arranged marriage between her and her applicant that she therefore passed to the house of her husband before the seven days expired.

For the client, she must go to her husband's house within seven days. The final ceremony can be arranged a day later, but it is very essential for the woman to be in the house of her husband within seven days to prevent her death

185

untimely This is very essential.

 Ikú won o d'ójó;
Àwon Àrùn won ò d'Ósù;
Díá fún Motóógbé;
Tíí s'omo Oníkàá; Mo
tóó gbé;
E wáà gbé mi o;
Bí oko ò lówó lówó;
Àlè won a nì;
Mo tóó gbé;
E wáà gbé
mi ì.

Translation:
Death never notifies
Afflictions never notify
These were Ifá's statement to Motóógbé
(I am quite prepared for marriage)
who was the daughter of Oníkàá.
Come and seek my hand in marriage
If my boyfriend does not have money for marriage
my admirer will have
I am quite prepared for marriage
Please come and seek my hand in marriage

5- VOCABULARY AND DEFINITIONS

WHAT FOR PROFESSIONAL ETHICS, EVERYTHING MUST KNOW BABALAWO

1. From memory, a large part of the Ifá literary corpus.
a. Masterfully manipulate the instruments of the oracle of divination.
2. Must be a well-versed interpreter, of the metaphorical language typical of ancestral literature.
3. Know exhaustively, the fauna and flora of your country and the therapeutic and magical utility of a large number of plants.
4. Know the fundamental ideograms (Odù de Ifá) and the incantations inserted in them.
5. You must constantly raise your level of theological and scientific information.

"In Ifá there is not everything, in Ifá everything fits".

This serves as a universal data bank where all existing existential events are stored, classified in the Ifá code.

"The true way to know nothing is to want to learn everything at once"

Ògbè Òdí

SOME ESSENTIAL ELEMENTS FOR THE INTERPRETATION IN THE ACT OF DIVINATION.

Ká firè fún ----- Finish comforting.

A dífá fún ------ He was in search of divination.

Lodá fún ------- You will perform the divination.

Mo firè fún ---- Òsà that we must take as a behavioral reference (her example or behavioral pattern in history or pataki that she refers to).

Abo fún -------- Who is close to the consulted.

Ajogún --------- Bad spiritualities (Death, illness, loss, etc.)

Ayanmó (Añamó) --- Destiny.

Áyewo (Ayeo)   Hex.

Ké fèrí lorí..........Incredulous.

Kán Kán lòní -------- Quickly, today, right now.

Kí nnkan má şe ---- Protect from evil forces.

Kó le ni ó díwo (Koleniodio) --- It shouldn't be occupying you all the time.

Jálè------------   Complete.

Mo jálè ---- Continue further.

Kòtó jálè --- It is insufficient, follow it or complete it.

é ko yes ---- Begging for something that is not there (is something missing?).

Laarí ìṣé òrìṣà? ------ Is a job with Òṣà important?

Ní torí, Intórí ------- Because of.

Lésè -------- At the foot of, follow the trail. Lówó ------- at the hands of.

Igbó -------- Forest, mone, manigua.

Ode..........Hunter.

Dáfá..........Divination.

SOME IRÉ E IBI (OSOBO) IMPORTANT

IRÉ

Iré aikú --------------------- Health benefit and long life

Iré àṣẹ́ gun ----------------- Benefit to win or conquer

Iré àṣẹ́ gun ọ̀tá ------------ Benefit from defeating enemies

Iré aya --------------------- Profit from a wife

Iré deedeewántòloòkun -Benefit of coming and going to the sea, fishermen, merchants

Iré omaa -------------------Intelligence benefit

Iré ìrìnkiri (inikini) -------- Travel benefit

Iré lésè eegún ------------ Benefit at the foot of the dead

Iré lésè ẹléda ------------- Benefit at the foot of the creator

Iré mérin layé ------------ Benefit that comes from the four parts of the world

Iré nlọlé siwaju ------------Benefit of improving by going to another land

Iré nṣowó (Iré ṣowo) ---- Profit of doing business

OSOBO (IBI)

Afitibó --------- Unexpected death

Akóba --------- Unexpected punishment, an unforeseen evil

Àroye............Complaint

Àrùn (anu).......Disease

Ejo (eyo)..........Judgment

Ikú..............Death

Iyan (iña) ----- Hunger, famine, etc.

Òfo ------------- Irreconcilable loss, divorce, differences

Òràn (ona) ----Big problem

Ònà ----------- leather, bumps

ELEMENTS OF DIVINATION FOR COMMUNICATION WITH ORI (ÌBÒ)

Apadí (Akuadí) ---- Piece of porcelain slab, opposite to iré.

Apa (Akua) --------- Bull's-eye Seed (beat opponents).

Gúngún ------------- (death, deceased and conclude).

Igbin ----------------- Elongated snail (Ayé), means union.

Òtá ------------------ Small stone, longevity and war.

Owó ----------------- Double snail (cowries), currency, profit, acquire. Àwòran (Awona) --Small image of cloth or clay.

Àgbálùmò ----------.Caimito Seed, enjoy life

Efun ----------------- Cascarilla Ball, represents purity.

Eyin (eñi) ---------- Tooth of an animal, irreparable loss.

Isìn ------------------ Seed of the vegetable Cease, represents

Òrúnmìlà. Sáyò ----Guacalote seed, children and multiplicity of goods.

191

THREE ODÙ MAKE UP A "DETERMINING FIGURE OF IFÁ" WHEN THE ORACLE IS CONSULTED.

Considering that an event is given by a query that a person makes to the Ifá oracle. Three esoteric figures will be considered as a general rule, which from these events emerge to take into account:

The first reading is called: Odù Toyale Iwá (1680 stories; patakí; eses).

This Odù investigates and explains the destiny of the person and in turn represents their problems.

The second reading is called: Odù Okuta Kulá (1680 stories; patakí; eses).

This odù reaffirms in detail what is expressed in the Toyale, it speaks of the causes of the person's problem.

The third spread is called: Odù tomala belanşe (1680 stories; patakí; eses).

This odù reaffirms what was expressed by the previous ones and in turn provides various possible solutions to the person's problem.

There are also two others important odù to take into account: The Boyuto odù that is a kind of guardian odù of the Toyale odù and its writing results from the opposite writing of its encryption. And the odù Omotorun Iwa which is the odù formed by the union of the ends of the odù Toyale and the odù Tomala belanşe.

Each Odù is supposed to have 1680 of those stories related to him, and this along with those of the other odù, and each one of them is supposed to be known by the Bàbálawo who is the one who guesses and sacrifices, it is expected that he has it in memory, although we have not found any capable of that feat ......

Ifá Divination page 16 Willian Bascom (End of quote).

And we also find that some authors of works and writings specialized in these matters, agree with these criteria.

As each odù will have 1680 possible stories related to it, and with equal possibilities for all. Since the probabilities for the three odù are the same, that is; 256 times for each of the positions in a query to the Ifá oracle, that is: $256 \times 256 \times 256 = (256)^3 = 16,777,216$. (Sixteen million seven hundred seventy-seven thouSand two hundred sixteen). This means that there are the same possibilities for each event, if we divide 1 by the number of possibilities in the event, a figure will be so small that it tends to be considered or taken "as zero probability". It is evident that the result of this mathematical operation tells us that it is very unlikely that this same Ifá figure will be repeated for many consecutive events, taking into account that, for a certain figure, there is an intrinsically concatenation of ideas. Expressed and summarized in the odù of Ifá. For these reasons it is practically impossible for any human mind to be able to store, keep in its memory and at the same time process such a volume of information in a minimum of time or duration of a consultation, so that the consultant can be considered optimal conditions and ready, to give an adequate response to each of the issues that you face when consulting the Ifá oracle. Unless, you use modern search and information processing methods that are very fast and efficient. Only Olódùmaré its creator and Òrúnmìlà its interpreter, are able to achieve it efficiently. I suppose that a human being would have to live around 700 years of life, with a brain in optimal conditions to be able to achieve it.

SOME EXPRESSIONS YORÙBÁ

Béè̩ ni.- Yes.

Béè̩ kó / ó ti.- No.

E̩̩s̩é.- thanks to you (to a superior or someone older than you).

Ós̩e.- thank you (to someone younger than you).

Mo dupé.- I thank you.

To dupe.- We thank you.

Mo dupé̩ pupò̩.- I thank you very much.

To dupé̩ pupò̩.- We thank you very much.

194

Kò topic.- You are welcome / It is not mentioned / it is nothing.

Àlàáfíà.- Humbly greeting "be the Good", a way of greeting someone wishing them well at the same time.

Note: This greeting is best used between relatives or with people younger than you. It is not considered an acceptable greeting for an older person. In some cases, this may be the greetings used to greet and show respect to a priest of an Òrìsà, but when used in this way it is accompanied by a specific ritual gesture to distinguish it from a social greeting used between peers.

Ò dàbò.- Goodbye.

Note: This greeting is universally used among peers and is liked by the elderly.

Ẹ má bínú.- I'm sorry (to a superior or someone older than you).

Má bínú.- I am sorry (to a fellow man or someone younger than you).

Ẹ kò topic.- You are welcome / It is not mentioned / is nothing (to a superior or someone older than you).

Kò topic.- You are welcome / It is not mentioned / it is nothing (to a similar or someone younger than you).

¿Kí ni orúkọ rẹ.- What is your name?

195

Orúkọ mi ni.- My name is.

Note: It is generally considered improper to ask someone's name in Yoruba culture. The idea of introducing yourself greeting, but asking for your name is a concept of cultures foreign to the Yorùbá culture. The exception is when someone older than you ask for your name, this is considered acceptable.

Ẹ dide! - Get up (to a superior or someone older than you).

Ẹ jókòó.- Sit down (to a superior or someone older than you).

Dide! - Get up (to a peer or someone younger than you).

Jókòó.- Sit down (to a peer or someone younger than you).

Ẹ Madide! - Do not stand up (to a superior or someone older than you).

Ẹ má jókòó.- Do not feel (a superior or someone older than you).

Madide! - Do not stand up (to a peer or someone younger than you).

Má jókòó.- do not feel (like someone or someone younger than you).

Mo féràn rẹ.- I love him (a person, singular).

Mo féràn yin.- I love you (more than one person, plural).

Mo naa féràn rẹ.- I love him too (one person, singular).

Mo naa féràn yin.- (to more than one person, plural).

VOCABULARY USED

The list in the next section presents some forms commonly used in the Yorùbá language that are directly related to Òrìṣà or to the practice of Ifá.

Abo.- Female (indicates gender, does not speak of a woman).

Abòrìṣà.- A worshiper of the Òrìṣà, most often used in the Diaspora to signify someone who has received some basic initiations. This distinguishes that person from the rest of the community.

Àbọrú Àbọyè Àbọṣíṣẹ.- To be able to sacrifice / a prayer for the sacrifice to be heard To be able to sacrifice / a prayer for the sacrifice to be accepted To be able to sacrifice / a prayer for the sacrifice to manifest "Àbọrú, Àbọyè" is considered one of the appropriate greetings for a Babaláwo or Ìyánifá (initiated in Ifá). The priest will return the greeting of "Àbọṣíṣẹ." In many cases and the blessing will extend to the initiate return this greeting. This varies from priest to priest.

Àdìmú.- The food offered to the Ancestors and / or Òrìṣà.

Àdúrà.- Prayer.

Ako.- The male (indicates gender).

Àlàáfíà.- Greeting that means "be the Good", a way of greeting someone and wishing them well-being at the same time. See the important note below the greetings section.

Àṣẹ.- The life force; a common meaning; "The power to manifest" or "is for what".

Awo.- The mystery; a name for all the devotees of Òrìṣà; a name for an individual Òrìṣà priest; a term that identifies the religion of Ifá.

Àyèwò.- Research, often used instead of "Ibi" in divination to indicate the need to investigate the problems further.

Baba / Baba my.- Father / my father.

Babalórìṣá.- Male priest of Òrìṣà, often the father of spiritual children.

Cuje.- It is a fine rod made from the branches of the tree ("Rasca Barrigas")

Ẹbọ.- The sacrifice to offer. This can bc uscd to indicate the offering of blood to the Òrìṣà although in the Diaspora this is often used as a term indicative of generally offering something to the Ancestors and the Òrìṣà.

Éèrìndínlógún.- The name of the sacred Oracle of the initiates of ìrìṣà.

It also refers to the sixteen cowries used during divination; the translation speaks "twenty minus four" which illustrates the Yorùbá way of calculating certain numbers.

Èèwò.- The taboo.

Egbé.- Society or group of people, for example, Ẹgbẹ́ Ọ̀sun is a group of initiates of Ọ̀sun.

Èjè.- Blood.

Ẹmu opé.- The palm wine.

Epo Papua.- Red palm oil.

Ewé.- Leaves or herbs.

Ibi.- Bad luck, bad fortune.

Ìbọrì.- Ritually serve the head, praising and feeding one's Orí.

Idè.- The ankle bracelet, bracelet or necklace, refers to the sacred articles adorned with Òrìṣà beads, although it is more used in the Diaspora to indicate a bracelet of some kind.

Igbá.- Literally "the gourd", but it is often used to indicate a container filled with the sacred mysteries and the consecrated instruments of the Òrìṣà example, Igbá Ọ̀sun is Ọ̀sun, the sacred ritual container.

Ikin Ifá.- The sacred palm nuts used in the most important divination rituals.

Ilé.- Accommodation, house, describes a family from Òrìsà.

Ìlèkè.- Literally "the beads" but it is often used to refer to the sacred necklaces adorned with Òrìsà beads.

I'll go.- Good fortune, good luck.

Ìyá, Ìyá my.- Mother, my mother.

Ìyálórìsà.- Priest woman of Òrìsà, often the mother of spiritual children.

Obì abata.- The cola nut.

Obìrin.- Female or specifically a woman.

Odù Ifá.- The 256 signs or marks used in Ifá divination that represent the fundamental forces of creation in the universe, it is literally used as a reference to the body of Ifá.

Ọgbèrì.- Someone who has not received any kind of initiation into the mysteries of Òrìsà, a novice.

Ọkùnrin.- The male, specifically a man.

Olorisa.- An initiate of the Òrìsà man or woman. Sometimes this word is used to indicate someone who has been initiated into the mysteries of Òrìsà but has not been spiritually initiated through the rites of consecration.

Olúwo.- In Ifá this term can be applied to an Ifá priest. The general meaning of the word indicates a person who teaches religion. It may, in some cases, indicate a certain line within the Ifá priesthood.

Omì tútù.- Fresh water

Omìèrò.- Water with consecrated herbs, "tranquilizing water".

Ọmọ.- The child, after spring. This can be used to refer to the biological years of spiritual children.

Ọ̀pèlè.- The Ifá divination chain.

Òrí.- White cocoa butter.

Oríkì.- Name of praise or story; sometimes used as an invocation to the matter of the Oríkì.

Orin.- The song.

Orógbó.- The bitter cola nut.

Ọṣẹ Dúdú / Ọṣẹ Aládin.- The black soap.

Ọtí.- A general word for spirits or wine.

Owó.- The money.

Oyin.- Honey.

SOME TERMS

Ajagún - The Yoruba term for warriors like the Orişa of protection.

Ajogún - The Yoruba term for denying forces.

Babalawo - The priest with a high degree of knowledge within the religious structure of Ifá.

Eegún - Hereditary entities.

Egúngún - The society within the Yoruba cultural structure that communes with and maintains the traditional directives of the ancestors.

Ehin Iwa - The Yoruba term for after life and reincarnation.

Elegun - Those initiated priests and priestesses who are possessed with the Orişa.

Enìkejì - The Yoruba term for the guardian angel.

Eniyan Gidi - the Yoruba term for the authentic or true human being.

Idé - Sacred beads worn on the left wrist by Ifá devotees.

El llé-Ife - The ancient spiritual capital of the present Yoruba nation.

Ìmoyé - like wisdom

The Fá de Ìpìlé - The process of determining one's African origins, using the Ifá divination system.

Ìrùnmolè - The Yoruba term for divinities.

The Ìyáamí - A Yoruba term for witches (The Mothers).

The chestnut tree - The term applied to the societies of freedom established by the African captives escaped from the "New World". Technically, this word is Spanish and is used for sheep or cattle that have been lost.

Odù - The sacred text and the religious body of Ifá; that was named after the admired wife of Orunmila. Also, the term applied to the vessels containing the consecrated objects of the priests.

Odùdúwà - The patriarch of the current Yoruba nation that he established himself.

Ogbọní - The society of superiors within the present Yoruba cultural context, which maintains the connection with the Earth and the cultural forces of African society.

Olódùmarè - the Creator - God in the Yoruba cultural context.

O'lòrìṣà - The Beginning of the priest or priestess within the Yoruba religious structure.

Òrìṣà - The interpretation of Ifá, of energy forces that emanate from the Creator.

These evolutionary divinities are also declared anthropologically as cultural archetypes of light and avatars.

Òrúnmìlà - The prophet, established by the religious cult of Ifá.

ABOUT THE AUTHOR

Marcelo Madan born in 1944 in Santiago de Cuba. He comes from an Afro-Cuban family with deep religious roots. Consecrated in the orisha Ọbàtàlá since 1951. Awo of Orunmila, consecrated in Ifá as Babalawo by his godfather Ruben Pineda (Baba EjiÒgbè), since 1992. His paternal grandfather, Eligio Madan "Ifanlá" of slave parents brought from Africa and a native of Jovellanos in the province of Matanzas Cuba.

His maternal grandmother María Belén Hernández, a famous Iyalorisha from the city of Havana and consecrated in the orisha Ọbàtàlá. His father Eligio Madan Hernández Awo de Orunmila (Ògbè Owonrin) and consecrated in the orisha Oshun. His maternal grandmother, a famous Iyalorisha from the city of Santiago de Cuba. At the beginning of the forties and fifties Rosa Torrez "Shangó Gumí", who together with the famous babalorisha also son of Shangó Rinerio Pérez, Amada Sánchez and Aurora La Mar el Oriate Liberato and others, initiate the first settlement of orishas in that city; She is the granddaughter of Ma Braulia, a free woman who came from Africa. Veneranda Constanten, her mother, also consecrated in Ọbàtàlá (Ewin fún), she dedicated her whole life to religious work together with her mother, Rosa Torrez.

These are the deep ancestral roots of Marcelo Madan, which

allowed them, through his consecration from an early age, to acquire the knowledge to carry out his religious literary works. And since then, he has become one of the most important researchers of the "lukumises" religion in Cuba, publishing dozens of books, among which are: the "Treaties of Ifá, Synthesis of the odu of Ifá, Orish Collections, The Oracles of the Orishas, Pocket Manual for Santeros, Meals and Adimú for the Saints among others.